LOCKDOWN LETTERS

&

OTHER POEMS

LOCKDOWN LETTERS

&

OTHER POEMS

PAUL MARION

LP

Loom Press
Lowell & Amesbury
Massachusetts
2021

ISBN 978-1-7351689-4-4

Printed in the United States of America
First edition

Design: Joseph Marion, www.MarionNYC.com
Author photograph: UMass Lowell
Printing: King Printing Co., Inc.
Text set in Cooper BT & Recife

Loom Press
P.O. Box 1394, Lowell, MA 01853
& 15 Atlantic View, Amesbury, MA 01913
www.loompress.com
info@loompress.com

Many of these compositions first appeared, sometimes in different
versions, in magazines, journals, blogs, anthologies, chapbooks, and
books, including *The Acre, Apple Tree Review, Bohemian (Japan),
Café Review, Fan: A Baseball Magazine, The First Yes: Poems About
Communicating, Generator Room, Hampden-Sydney Poetry Review,
Hit Singles, Line Drives: 100 Contemporary Baseball Poems,
The Lowell Review, Middle Distance, The Offering, PaulMarion.com,
PoetsReadingtheNews.com, Point West, Red Brick Review,
RichardHowe.com, San Fernando Poetry Journal, South Coast Poetry
Journal, So It Goes* (Kurt Vonnegut Museum & Library), *SpoKe Seven,
Sport Literate, St. Andrews Review, Strong Place: Poems '74-'84,
Visiting Frost: Poems Inspired by the Work and Life of Robert Frost,
What Is the City?,* and *Wisconsin Review: 25th Anniversary Issue.*
"The Storks of Alsace" is forthcoming in *So It Goes.*

For everyone in the time of the virus

Contents

LOCKDOWN LETTERS

GRAND TOUR

WISH YOU WERE HERE

LESSER ANTILLES

CHERRY TOMATOES

MARTIAN CANALS

A DREAM OF PERFECT GAMES

Make Words

"If there were a lake, the swans would go there."
—*The Black Hat Lama in Boston*

Make words for the uninitiated, those in the other room,
For the woman in the city selling brooms,
For copper fields and gold woods,
For technology's ghost, the stick in the spokes.
Make words for blood ties, thicker as the years go,
For the red giant starburst we'll never find,
For the illimitable silence of the deep white sound,
The slumberous humming bay.

Make words for biomes and prestidigitation,
For bicycle synergism,
For the enormous lovers, the enormous learners,
For the common bones of life.
Make words for a kitchen full of poets,
For sawdust on the rug,
For computers without bugs,
For the healthiest meal on TV.

Make words for wise acquisition,
For the ax buried near the oak,
For searchlights panning the sun,
For having no idea what we know.
Make words for spirit fatigue and the early return,
For the attempt to cultivate brevity,
For the community that holds your stake,
For those swans going to a lake.

Recordings

Beware of common sense
  Sun & moon look the same size
Galileo insisted that Earth circles the sun
  Described wine as air bound by light
Aristotle saw heavenly bodies as perfect
  Earth as imperfect, at rest

You must submit to vulgarity
  Or cease to be the First Minister
Lady Glencora told Plantagenet Palliser
  Try to coexist with the hornets

Our business is with life, not death
  The challenge is to give what account
We can of what becomes of life
  In the solar system, this corner of the Universe
That is our home, and, most of all
  What becomes of us, said George Wald

"Wear a mask."

—Dr. Anthony Fauci

Lockdown Letters

In July 2020, I composed "Lockdown Letters," reframing email messages to friends sent at the start of the pandemic. The mash-up of email and slant-sonnet gave me a closed form, even if not strict structure, in the midst of the random slashing damage of a virus that takes down one person and leaves another standing.

Feb. 29, 2020. In Seattle, Washington, authorities report the first coronavirus death in the United States. Global infections reach 87,000. Americans are urged not to travel to northern Italy and South Korea.

March 7 (to Marie and Dick)

Turn the clock ahead. Tomorrow, with Ree,
I'll see Chath and Ken at their farm in Bolton
For a walk in the orchard and a Thai meal.
I'm worried about my upcoming book launch
For the anthology of Cork and Lowell writers,
Figuring the virus will worsen each day and
People will avoid getting together. The drama
Reminds me of a pulpy science-fiction movie
With breaking-news flashes about another
Flying saucer landing in Budapest, two more
In Pakistan, and now Scotland blacked out.
The President sounds stupid as he bullshits
His way through the crisis and spins info
As if this disease is simply bad ink for him.

March 8 (to Dick)

The news about the virus rots, and
Stocks and oil prices fell again. It'd
Be easy to shut the blinds and stay in,
But we're going to the farm. Last night,
Mike in Eagle River, Alaska, by way of
Haverhill, sister river city, sent me a
Memory piece for your blog, about the
Commodore Ballroom, his first big show,
The Young Rascals tearing up the place
In '71. He added that he and his wife fled
Washington state where she had surgery—
The virus spread scaring them. I asked
Him to write a Covid-19 update for you
From his vantage point in the Northwest.

March 10 (to John W. and Denis)

I picked up our new anthology at King Printing.
Atlantic Currents is a beauty. Air freight will take
Three to five days to Cork, door-to-door. One
Of our contributors, Bob H., a one-time elite
Runner with a new memoir, gave the *Lowell Sun*
An interview in which he plugged *AC*. Denis,
I'm sorry the virus mugged Cork's Learning City
Festival. Our author-palooza set for April
Might get sidelined, too. Massachusetts
Declared a State of Emergency, expanding the
Governor's power in this public health crisis.
Schools can fix schedules in each community's
Best interest. Authorities lifted the 185-day
Requirement for the academic year. Extreme.

March 13 (to Fred)

This emergency feels vastly consequential.
Our nation will be altered in body-and-soul when
We-the-people come out the other side of this,
The lucky ones with butts intact, maybe by Fall.
We'll be at risk until a vaccine is ready. I hope
The citizens keep their cool collectively. In four
To six weeks the infection count will skyrocket
As tests reveal more sickness. The N.Y. Gov.
Sealed off New Rochelle (pop. 70,000),
Directing the National Guard to keep order.
If the GOP Senators had spines, they would
Force the President to resign, and with Dems
Create a public-health oversight council to enact
A Whole-of-Government response to the crisis.

March 13 (to Marie and Dick)

We've reached the moment when an intervention
Must happen in the White House. The President
Endangers the public each day he remains in office
Without any idea how to get out of this trouble. He's
Overmatched by the virus, no surprise given that
He's the hoax, one of his favorite trash-bombs, a fake
President, cheesy Reality TV star who pulled off
The greatest con in U.S. politics. Let him plead sickness
And hand the nuclear codes to the Vice President, not
A world-beater himself, but less of a raw danger to us.
Such a drastic move could shock the national psyche
Back to a certain stability. The monied class shouts
Its lack of confidence. Japan's market dove ten percent.
How many 2000-point Dow losses tolerated at home?

March 14 (to Steve)

I grew up with your former teaching colleague Bob,
Whose house was across from mine on the diagonal.
His dad was an engineer at Raytheon Missile Systems
In Lowell or Andover. In the early 1960s, around the
Time of the Cuban Missile Crisis, his dad built a plain
Fallout shelter in the basement or maybe just off it
Like a reinforced bulkhead. Only once did I see inside,
During a birthday party for his brother—a blond sister
Was the youngest of three kids. The concrete-block
Shelter contained blankets, paper plates, canned goods,
A toolbox (am I making this up?), water bottles, and
More basic supplies. What did his dad know? At school,
We did duck-and-cover drills downstairs, crouching
Under baby-grade desks until Sister Irene's all-clear signal.

March 14 (to Victoria)

Rosemary and I wish you ecstatic days and nights.
We saw the wedding photos taken by the Lowell
Gang that flew to Northern Ireland. Please send
Your street address so I can ship an author's copy
Of *Atlantic Currents*, which you'll enjoy. Thank you,
For giving us a part of the novel-in-progress, your
Smashing prequel to labor chief Hugh C.'s Lowell tale.
We cancelled our book launch due to the plague.
Cork friends put off the yearly Learning City fest,
Where they planned to unveil the book on April one.
I hope this mess clears by September, and that we've
Made it to the other side. If so, we will gather to
Celebrate here and I hope with friends near you.
I look forward to your finished book and a bash.

March 15 (to Dick)

I keep getting texts from Bernie S., which feel
Superfluous in the face of Covid. He's trying hard
To regain his footing vs. Joe Biden. What do you make
Of the postponed primaries, Louisiana and Georgia?
Is this a preview of Republican moves to delay
The general election due to the virus? I wouldn't
Put it past them to try. The lead article in *Atlantic* mag
Grimly tracks the President's victories against a
Phantom Deep State, all those career civil servants.
He's downed federal agencies like he buried multiple
GOP opponents in 2016, revealing the scant courage
Among bureaucrats with pensions. He's a master bully,
Backed by Senator Moscow Mitch and the nasty AG.
The generals who left him should tell the truth.

March 16. Venezuelans quarantine. Ecuador and Peru lock down. New York City closes its schools. U.S. doctors say it's okay to meet in groups of no more than ten.

March 17 (to Ben)

Are you and Sue leaving Florida in hazmat suits?
We have to keep a sense of humor about the plague.
Speaking of New England, Tom Brady is moving.
Is he undermining himself, bound to stumble like
Aged Willie Mays in the New York Mets outfield?
You have to know when to exit. Two years ago,
He might've quit as a champ. Now he persists,
A step slower at forty-three, grasping for what?
He's done it all. The media say few teams chased him
In his free-agent cape. And this comes amid the corona
That's tipped over the table of overpaid athletes, exposing
How not vital they are compared to newly discovered
Essential workers: truck drivers, grocery cashiers, letter
Carriers, water-plant techs, and medical staff of all kinds.

March 17 (to Jane)

Yes, Portland seems a half-year ago, psychically. Hope
You can write that piece about your dad's memory of
The 1918 Influenza and your research. Just back from
The supermarket where people robot-walked the aisles,
A change from two days ago. No bright eyes, a searching
Look like tornado survivors. But we are not "there" yet,
In immediate danger, at least it doesn't feel like it. The
Threat is invisible, insidious in a way that a flood or
Twister is not. I imagined people's brains clicking:
What can I buy that'll last? They want bread to freeze
And bathroom tissue. The bread section was mostly
Empty. And no paper products. Not a square of tissue.
I then stopped at Vermette's (staples and beer/wine),
Where single rolls of TP are rationed, two per human.

I got my rolls and a bag of cat litter. At Stop & Shop,
I'd bought items to send to my son Joe in Brooklyn.
He's working at home for his (not his own) Wall St.
Ad firm. Today, he wrote a billboard pitch about virus
Precautions for a Catholic medical center in New Jersey.
Rich retirees are flying to Tampa to beat the spread.
We're lucky to have a comfortable base. On the web
From Italy, I scanned pages of obituaries, those lost
So far in one city of 100,000. Weeks ago, American
Travelers were warned to avoid northern Italy.

The nightly reports are brutal. In beautiful Milan,
Which Rosa and I toured last summer, everything
Is closed—one side benefit being cleaner air
While the cars, taxis, and trucks stay parked.

March 18 (to Dick)

I ordered Heather Cox Richardson's new book,
How the South Won the Civil War. I don't expect an
Uplifting read, but I've become a big fan of hers
Through her daily "Letters from an American,"
A rundown of events with a view that appeals
To me—she's for the Enlightenment and not the
Dark Ages. I can guess what's inside, but I'll surely
Learn something. What I'm wondering is: How do I
Put in play, in a small way, what I'll pick up from her?
Even more now, I want to link ideas to action, which
I've always tried to do. The union, reduced to the local
Level, feels more at risk than in decades, virus or not.
Last night, I got nervous after coughing and feeling
My breathing was off. I'm alert to each shiver & twitch.

March 18 (to John W.)

Back from the morning forage along the river.
I snagged a roll of paper towels that was lodged
Under a failed freezer case at Stop & Shop and
Two pounds of carrots (plenty in the produce
Section), bagged veg two-for-the-price-of-one.
I'm making a chili concoction, not with carrots,
Between chili and a goulash, for the household pot.
Canned kidney beans are handy. I mailed six books
Today. I need the post office to stay open. As our
Contributors receive comp copies of the anthology,
They'll post the cover on Facebook, the best viz
Available in the virus fog. Cork should see its books
Any day. Let's hope somebody with a mask is around
To accept them at City Hall where Denis said to ship.

March 19. China reports no new locally based infections. In early January, scientists in Wuhan, China, announced they had found a new virus.

March 19 (to Dick)

I suggested to Paul H. that he make like Samuel Pepys
In old London and for your blog give an account of
The coronavirus from his perch atop Lord Manor at
Pawtucket Falls. He's intrigued. I suspect he may be
Doing this anyway. He sends me bits and pieces of his
Observations, insights, and varied reading notes.
Occurs to me that regular blog readers will respond.
Why not? It's a unique moment, at least for the past
Hundred years. Paul is hyper-aware of news, learn-ed,
Acutely attentive to his environment inside the seniors'
Housing complex and outside as seen from his windows
That offer a view of Pawtucket Street traffic in front of
The old Ayer Mansion, later Franco-American School,
Being renovated for apartments, and over to the falls.

March 22 (to Marie and Dick)

Without subscribing, I get updates from a few papers
In the U.S., including the *Chattanooga Times Free Press.*
Interesting today to see a page one lead story about
The "U.S." (not the President) being unprepared
For the virus. According to ABC News, fifty-five percent
Of persons surveyed approve of the President's handling
Of the virus (though he's underwater in some polls), a shock,
Considering the clusterfuck mega-botch of the pandemic.
Proves the benefit of keeping your face on TV and lying
About what happened in January-February in the run-up.
This rating will be key to watch as we head to summer,
And the fall election view sharpens. If the infection subsides
By August-September, the President will ride a white stallion
Ahead of a column of tanks down Pennsylvania Avenue.

March 23 (to Joe)

Governor Charlie Baker locked down Massachusetts
Until April 7. All non-essential businesses must close
Physical operations. Open: grocery stores and companies
That service food markets, pharmacies, gas stations, and
Banks with drive-up. The U.S. post office keeps rolling.
Delivery companies like UPS, FedEx, and Amazon open.
Transportation system OK: bus, train, light rail, subway.
People are not confined to home. Not shelter-in-place
Or a legal quarantine. More "like guidelines" as Barbossa
In *Pirates of the Caribbean* says about a "parley." Tall Baker
Stands like Steady Eddie at the podium each noontime.
He said, "Don't be a bonehead and play pick-up hoops
When you go outside." (He didn't use bonehead.) This
Is my report. Mum and I shipped you a box of stuff today.

March 25 (to John W.)

Joe holed up in Brooklyn. We asked if we should pick
Him up or if he wants to take Amtrak to Amesbury to
Visit for a week. New York decays by the hour. He's
Disciplined about staying in, working remotely. Goes out
For fresh air, sometimes runs two miles with mask & gloves.
Another week, and I think he'll be fed up. We send food,
And he gets deliveries of items that he can't buy at a bodega
Or another store nearby that has butter, milk, and ice cream.
Our book sells steadily. I'll soon post the antho on Amazon,
But want to sell more right from Loom Press to skip the deep
Discount demanded by the wide river of products in the sky.
I'm listening to Paul Simon's recent CD of lesser-known songs,
In the Blue Light. Love the one about the Magrittes & their dog.
Trump's insane dream of "opening up" for Easter will kill us.

March 25 (to Dave)

I like your story. I know the other Dave D. from a publishing
Project I did years ago when my friend Eric ran a bookstore
In Chelmsford. Weird that the same-name-guys crossed paths.
Neck-hairs stand up when I see a rack of new literary mags,
Imagining fresh words between covers. Never mind the few
Readers, I figure it's all done for Me. I envy your calorie-
Rich reading sessions at the Harvard Coop. I'll talk to Dick
About kicking off a feature like Book Day on his blog:
Invite literary posts, reading updates, what's on the night
Table like the *New York Times Book Review* weekly Q&A,
That sort of thing. Chath said he's being considered for
A national poetry prize in Cambodia—this deserves attention.
I have his manuscript that's due from my press next year,
But I can rush the production. Doing my dream job.

March 26. The U.S. now leads the world in Covid-19 cases with more than 81,000 people infected and 1,000 dead from the virus. This week, India suspended all domestic plane travel.

March 26 (to George)

The flowers on the piano or worse,
The idea of flowers on a conceptual piano.
One time in America poets were heroes.
Whittier's *Snow-Bound* topped $10,000 in royalties.
There's not a bag of frozen peas to be had.
Things that felt so necessary lack urgency.
Graphs in Covid briefings are applied math
For shut-in school kids. Do the numbers.
Misplaced gerunds. Make a note.
The Grand Budapest Hotel is a grand confection.
The radiating effects will be substantial
When Chath's new book achieves "sticky."
Imagine if the virus had burst in winter,
Made fiercer by the road ice and snow.

March 26 (to Elisha)

At just light the folded news in a plastic sleeve
Lands slap on my driveway, tossed by the analog
Town-crier carrier whose car doesn't stop
At every house the way I recall the paper
Delivered by kids on bikes in my hometown.
Our up-the-street hill wasn't as angled
As this longtime ski slope now topped
By townhouse condos, a small cluster
On the crest visited by foxes, skunks, deer,
And hometown birds, checking back in
This spring, at least those who fled the cold,
Ruby-throated and sky blue-chested, welcome
To our balcony perch facing gray-brown hills
In New Hampshire and a distinct Maine peak

To the northeast—the top of the rise here
Named by custom for tribal grounds, hundreds,
Thousands of years ago, forest time, lake time,
High water pushing a slim, feisty river
Through the downtown re-made mill yard:
Offices, hardware mecca, studios, flatbread
Pizzeria, pubs, apartments, and coffee shop,
Whose beating-dollar heart is a good sign
This spring on the local front where most
Citizens want a safe-and-sound routine,

Not too much to ask in days when news
Of the universe carries more pain and chaos
Than are helpful to us and to our dogs and
Cats, neighbor birds, and the close red fox.

March 29 (to Marie and Dick)

I'm picturing the near-term. People can't be confined
Indefinitely. That said, infection cases increase in-state
As testing shows a determined virus. There's a Medieval
Mysteriousness in the way the germ "selects" victims.
Surprising. Brutal. Out of the virus fog a case emerges.
UMass Lowell blasted a message from the Chancellor
Saying a few people at the university are infected.
No number—only detail is it's not a student living
On campus. Staff and faculty in contact with those
Infected got warned. In a New Jersey nursing home,
Ninety residents, the entire roster, tested positive.
Rosemary is reupholstering the dining-table chairs.
Tedious to pull scores of brittle staples from stiff fabric
That wraps around the chair bottoms. We have the time.

April 2. Worldwide, the coronavirus has sickened more than one million people and killed more than 50,000. In America, 6.6 million workers signed up for unemployment benefits last week, ten times more than any week in national history.

April 3 (to John S.)

We're worried about Joe as New York City deteriorates.
He's buttoned up in Bedford-Stuyvesant and has food—
Fortunate that he got two large deliveries a week ago
Because it's chaos trying to schedule something now.
We send cartons of basics & extras via post office
Every three days, which so far are delivered efficiently.
Don't know how he'd leave—he could Uber to Penn Station,
Take Amtrak north, or go to his girlfriend's place in Jersey.
One of his ad clients is a medical center in Teaneck,
Which makes him feel part of the "war." Mayor de Blasio
Ordered New Yorkers to wear masks when outside.
Joe has cotton bandanas. I'll send him a primo mask.
He told us not to worry—he could be on duty in Afghanistan.
Pelting rain here all day. Off-shore storm with gusty winds.

April 4 (to Jane)

Good to hear from you. Glad you're safe. We're masked.
I have two "elite" masks of the N95 type, which I bought
To clean our old house—and carried them to Amesbury.
I covered up and wore plastic gloves at the superette,
Where five people are let in at a time per Health Board.
At home, we're well stocked and won't have to shop again
For a couple of weeks. We buy milk and eggs down the hill.
Is this where the situation will stay for a while, most people
Obeying authorities and adjusting to a civic control system
For buying food and medicine? Will we see an inflection point
In thirty days if the sickness keeps spiking and people panic?
Federal rescue bill money won't reach everyone in time or
Be nearly enough for an extended crisis. Emotions will fray.
I read that Italy has a slight downward curve in deaths.

The stay-home order will help doctors catch up to
Undiagnosed folks at large. We're buffered here
With fewer people, dispersed. City infection rates rise.
GOP bosses back the President no matter the damage,
Confident they'll be rewarded, politically, financially.
Horrific to watch the national effort. Are you volunteering
At the food bank? I'm glad the *Georgia Review* pulled your essay
On the 1918 Influenza from its archive for new readers.
Regarding the South, I heard media grandees Howell Raines
Of Alabama, former *N. Y. Times* editor, and Walter Isaacson

In New Orleans talking about the virus in their region.
Margaret Renkl today writes about Tennessee and the storm
Set to whack rural states. We walk Ringo-the-dog to the top
Of our hill with its view of the Maine highlands south of you.

April 5 (to Suzanne)

In the time of the virus, every other Wednesday
Marie concocts pasta stew with ground beef,
Elbows, chopped tomatoes, onions, green peppers,
Crushed garlic, and a jar of branded red sauce,
Filling a deep stainless pan—
Her slumgullion will last the week,
Better reheated on the stove or given a second life
Topped with sliced cheese in the oven. We've all
Been home-cooking in the long lockdown,
Stirring up favorites and thumbing through Julia's book,
Watching Jacques Pépin's quick videos via laptop,
Lifting tips from the *Boston Globe* food writers.
Our sharp knives get a workout. No need to rush.
This dish could use a little hot sauce, too.

April 8 (to Tom)

The blue ox rests in the trunk of my car. Inflatable.
Fill him at the gas station to make an impression.
I keep asking people, Is this as bad as it will get here?
The number of infected persons of all ages goes up,
And the death count hovers, not a big jump day to day.
Nursing homes being clobbered, old-soldier posts ravaged.
How does the almighty germ get under the door?
What's happening near you and Sharyn in Alaska?
Sometimes this drama seems like a bad cartoon
With a smoke trail of poison slithering hither.
From the clearing atop our ancient tribal hill,
I look at the line where the Atlantic Ocean meets sky.
Big fat moon tonight around the world. Bounced light.
We must reflect each other's light to outshine the darkness.

July 19, 2020. Massachusetts reported 114,000 confirmed cases of Covid-19 and 8,431 deaths from the disease to date.

(Timeline data courtesy of *The New York Times*)

Grand Tour

Rhine Swim

Bells at five on the Rhine, running silver-blue
North to Mannheim and Nijmegen,
This hot slow Sunday, late August in Basel,
Where the banks are fleshed bridge to bridge
And past my view—the good citizens soaking.
One of them enters the water each minute,
Adding to the flotilla of loafers and focused jocks
In the ritual float or swim, most with a sealed red bag,
The *wickelfisch*, bobbing ahead, a freelance buoy,
Its clothes, phone, and wallet aiming for Strasbourg,
But bathers stop long before France and swim to land
To repeat while sun warms the wall where folks combine,
Watching out for each other, no lifeguards in sight,
The authorities on season break in the Italian hills.

Names of Barges

After Donald Hall and his horses

Theodela, Vianen, Maersk, Werner Reich, Votesse, Synthesis 6,
Rhinekrone, Andrea II, Inversa, AnneRose, Mejora, Rhemus.

Like Mark Twain in his Heidelberg cap at the controls,
Captain Greta guides the ship with the current seaward,
Her vessel overloaded with the fraught freight of all of us,
Pushing past Twain's quaint Rhine Gorge castles and traces
Of pirate toll-takers, past the ramparts and princess spires,
Just not funny these days, not a distraction that Greta
Can abide, all business as she strikes forward, using nature
To reveal Nature and yelling at us from the bridge,
"The house is on fire!" (unsaid, You stupid old fools!).

Marcona, Kohl-Düsseldorfer, Hyundai, Tramp, Inga II, Valetta,
Oscar Wilde Basel, Amakristina, Ella Rotterdam, Evident, Till.

And the barges line up behind her lead, heading away
From the highlands and towards open water where hot cargo
Can be cooled and cleaned by windmills and salted water,
The lock-tenders alerted to the convoy, the water levels enough
This summer to satisfy the pilots, not like last July when boys
Played football in the dry bed, the expensive tours cancelled,
The burning air killing the weak and poor in Toulouse,

Before the Yellow Vests in Paris streets said, We can't worry
The world's ending when we try to live to the end of the month.

Lorely Elegance, Marktheidenfeld, Chateau Chalon, Stolt Maas,
Terra Nova, Virginia, Springer, Gerhard Schmitter, Ina, Damina-K.

German *Easy Rider*

On the ship's TV with Rhine River black outside closed drapes
Scenes shine like color pages of LIFE magazine hippie spreads
By 1969 scribes who sniffed the grass on tie-dyed trails
To communes like the desert crib that Peter Fonda studies,
A Margaret Mead-anthropologist, but in his back yard,
Not the South Seas, the natives with blond hair, and
He's curious about the sex part of the cave set-up—
His hopped-up Hopper sideman leering and lapping it,
Twirling in Davy Crockett buckskins, fringe doing a dance
For the women of the house. We don't see Jack N. in this part,
Being featured tonight as a link to Fonda's recent death,
Fifty years to the movie's summer and moon-men landing,
In time for Woodstock tales (anniversary concert plug
Pulled last minute), same theme in the City Museum of
Amsterdam, a media piece bragging on the loose-life vibe

Of San Francisco and Amsterdam, then Freak World capitals,
The Netherlands famously drawing the famous Two Virgins
For a hotel bed-in peace advert, same Fonda who told John
(You know him) at an L.A. party that he, Peter, knew what it's like
To be dead, which we later heard on *Revolver*, the party a bit
Before Joan Didion sensed the American Center wasn't holding,
Although she may've been melodramatic, given what we know
Fifty years later—that the music had a hold on us and hasn't let go,
The music beat time, witness Zap Records in downtown A-dam

With its fat bin of Beatles vinyl, first on the left when you enter,
A fact to like in the German night cruising the Rhine towards
Düsseldorf and watching *Easy Rider* dubbed and without
English subtitles, which doesn't matter, just look at the picture,
Wait for the sticky music and bloody ending, no translation needed—
No editor's-cut resurrection for Wyatt and Billy in the rerun.

Route to War and Back (a notebook)

[In the winter and early spring of 1945 my soldier-father helped defeat the Nazis, the fascists, on the ground in Europe. Seventy-four years later, my wife and I traveled through parts of Germany, and I felt strange walking where he had walked. Time collapsed, and history pulsed. In a notebook, he recorded his path to the war and his return. Dad spoke very little about what happened to him in Europe, a few stories of being in danger. He didn't march in parades at home. He always wanted to see Paris and Bavaria, again, but died before he had a chance.]

Marcel R. Marion, Fourth Division, US Army, WWII Service

Oct. 3, 1944, Camp Devens, Mass.

Oct. 13, Camp Blanding, Fla.

Jan. 30, 1945, 11 days delaying route

Feb. 9, Fort Meade, Md.

Feb. 10-12, Three-day pass to Lowell, Mass.

Feb. 14, Camp Kilmer, N. J.

Feb. 18, Queen Mary ocean liner

Feb. 25, Gourock, Scotland (British berth for Queen Mary)

[My father has Glasgow written here, but I think it's a mistake. Amazingly, the ocean liner troop transport schedules are online, which show N.Y. to Gourock leaving Feb. 19]

Feb. 25, Southampton, England

Feb. 27, Le Havre, France

[The spellings are tricky both because of handwriting and him guessing at place name spellings.]

Toul, France

Tergnier, France

Luxembourg

Jeffenhurk, Germany

St. Vith, Belgium

Prum, Germany

Hildersheim

Nancy, France

Brimarsh, France

Thionville, France

Lunéville, France

Worms, Germany

Wurzburg

Bazooka Town, Germany

Grünsfeld

Bad Mergentheim

Rothenburg

Crailsheim

Heidenheim

Augsburg

Nuremburg

Munich

Tegernsee

Roth

Dinkelsbühl

Kaiserslautern

Metz, France

Soissons

Le Havre

Newport News, Va.

Camp Patrick Henry, Va.

Fort Devens, Mass.

July 24, 1945

Camp Burton, N.C.

Points: 38

45-day furlough pending

Covered about 24,000 miles in my Army career

Feb. 17, 1946

Discharged

The Storks of Alsace

So many of them
Shocked on power poles
When their big feet
Touched live wires
Or snagged mid-flight
On electric lines,
Which clunky wings
Could not clear,
So many birds killed
By modernity that
Residents built nests,
Half-ton baskets atop
Town hall, fire station,
The library and school,
Stick bowls on platforms,
Wide as a kiddie pool,
Message on the skyline—
We saw a bird upright,
One of one thousand
In the last civic count,
The special-guest fliers
Eyeing our passing bus
Headed to a Green winery,
Domaine Achillée, near Colmar.

Paris Glass

1.

Near Sainte-Chapelle, a seated old woman with short black
hair shows us two fluffy rabbits, white-and-brown, on leashes
at her spot of sidewalk mid-bridge where she has a pile of
greens, two cups of pellets, and water in a shiny silver bowl.

2.

On a black iron church fence on Blvd. St.-Germain a poet-
painter offers a line of monotypes, colored abstractions,
stylized landmarks accented with words by Apollinaire,
Neruda, Rimbaud, Rilke, lyric slivers of emotion and insight,
his pop-up gallery in the boundless market.

3.

Making our way down the guidebook trail past the Voltaire
statue, house of George Sand, and then the toy store linked
to *Le Petit Prince* and Babar the Elephant, the hand-written
notice: "*Fermé Lundi*," dark interior, select playthings on the
inside window ledge, plastic city figures, fire fighters and
soccer stars.

4.

Palais de Justice surrounding virtuoso stained-glass, and the
Gendarmerie forces all about the wide courthouse steps close
to St. Louis chapel with its high windows as bright as diced
fruit at mid-morning.

5.

See-through boats as long as trains filled with white cloth-
covered tables for four going north on the Seine, greenish
brown, sliding past the bookstalls where casual tenders
hawk vintage film magazines, fugitive pop culture posters,
tiers of paperbacks in French and Euro languages, the stalls
like big lidded tea tins mounted on cement walls above the
river, the shelves, racks, and spinners dense with Marlon
Brando, Picasso, Led Zeppelin, Camus, Obama, and Monet
prints, portraits of Princess Di, rare Simone de Beauvoirs,
cat pins, Madonna postcards, Napoleon pennants, stained
cookbooks.

6.

Icy green-glass bottles of Coca-Cola delivered two and four
at a time by waiters to smoking models, lunch loafers, and
graybeards in jeans and leather waist-jackets, sitting side-
by-side, drinking wine and touching shoulders like men in
Omaha, Nebraska, would never do, all the citizens tucked
into their Café Palette tables filled with plates of sumptuous
roasted whole legs of chicken on rice beds, the couscous
special, yolked ham-and-cheese *croque-madames*, baby
spinach with a mustard-honey dollop, and sparkling water,
not still, this fizzy afternoon on the Left Bank.

7.

Nine hundred years, Notre Dame de Paris, in a land where
eight of ten churches are tributes to Mary Mother of
Catholic-God's Son; the hard gargoyle, hands a-ears, won't
hear St. Denis's severed head scream to warn about the
devil's movement on Mary's shoulder; a fair sample of the
world lined up outside, Swedish and Chinese guests doing
the selfie thing at Point Zero, brass disk from which radiate
concentric cultural waves.

8.

La Tour Eiffel, tan as a desert rat and peeling on the sun side
from a bad and outsourced paint job, the surface muted in
daylight, matching neighborhood architecture, sand, earth,
stone, olive, gray, a blend of neutrals almost like a trick in the
City of Light, as subtle as the Sahel peddlers with dozens of
small twinkling towers spread on sheets which get hauled
up by four corners and slung over shoulders in two seconds
when the police pull up, the vendors all of a sudden just St.
Nicks in Nikes, "Nothing to see here, move along, nobody
selling, displays only, no problem, everybody wants a tower,
everyone needs a light."

9.

Figs and mushrooms and strawberries displayed like museum pieces that can be touched. Brilliant oranges from South Africa piled up for squeezing, orange oil perfuming the intersection. Baguette sandwiches in hashtag stacks. The cheeses sit by their names, waiting to be called on and not saying a word to the salamis.

10.

Hemingway's favorite writing place in Saint-Germain-des-Prés. There. No, over there. No, no, it's across the street for sure. He drank there all the time.

Duomo di Milano

Early during the Covid-19 quarantine, a news photo
of the plaza fronting the Milan cathedral, the *Duomo di Milano*,
shows a masked man with two dogs and many birds,
maybe the same pigeons Rosemary and I saw last summer
landing on the arms of tourists to eat popcorn sold by hawkers
who work with pickpocket pals, expert at the bump-and-run
just as the pigeon-mass wheels up, bursting like a grenade
when one acute flier among them signals "Go!"

Chased by a strong germ, the local citizens
have scattered back behind doors, some nights singing
with neighbors through open windows or on balconies
above empty streets. The tourists went away
and may not return for a long time. In the chorus,
the spunky servers, *barista*, and *chef di cucina*
from the trattoria where we lingered one night.

On a plaza as wide as the church is tall, we joined sightseers
mixed with believers, moving but almost not moving, so packed,
across the paving stones. For three Euros women choose scarves
draped over forearms of vendors outside pay-as-you-go toilets
alongside the cathedral, only one Euro for a flush and hand gel.

Women cannot enter the *Duomo* with bare shoulders
even ten centuries after the marbled "failure" of mottled white,

(Oscar Wilde's take, not mine, but I get his point),
a pile-up of steeples, flutes and flourishes, holy figures,
angels on high, Mary-tributes, stacked tip to top,
a giant gaudy birthday cake studded with candles
from which have dripped chalky coating, time-stopped,
one thousand years of prayers, and still standing—
a disco diva outside La Scala singing to the soft blue sky
when we returned in small groups to our air-cooled bus.

Great Lake

Lago Maggiore out the left windows on the train from Basel
Which stops eight times before monumental Milan station.
Past tunnels, long and short, the view is waterside, islands,
A great lake, its size not a surprise as I've been tracking
By phone, global position in hand, blue lengthening when I
Scroll up on the screen, no end in sight, coordinates sprayed
Earthward from satellites, updating, south-land unrolling,
No bottom, for the map rolls north at the pole, the image
Stored in a cloud or super-drive, land scanned for all-purpose,
For armies and authors and Auntie Mame on a Grand Tour,
Directions easy to follow across all known borders, places
Flat on-screen like paper photographs or carved stone,
Except digital-green, -blue, and -brown—signs, marks
On the way, code to where we are and want to go.

The Last Supper

We arrived in a group twice the size of the Apostles,
Not more due to controls, like an airlock to dehumidify us,
Precautions for the painting, its supper table more like a stage
With figures stopped at the words said in that district,
Challenges to oldsters and guides used to owning the show,
Not thrilled with an interloper, holier-than-thou, said to have
Powers of a comic-book hero, a carpenter's kid from Nazareth
Sitting in the center with companions leaning in and away,
Triggered by what he has said, the forecast of betrayal;
One will front-stab, and the men, middle-aged or younger,
Followers of this new form of man who told loaded stories—
These guys had no idea about what was coming.

What was I doing in front of Leonardo's masterpiece?
Just outside, people walk their dogs, ride bicycles,
Chat in pairs. There's no sign with an arrow aiming at
An icon of Western Civilization, no line-up of armed cops,
No landscaped entrance. Inside the simple meeting hall—
With a Crucifixion scene on one wall, not by Leo the engineer,
Who messed up the paint mix on his late-delivered tableau
And caused endless restoration—inside we looked and looked
And took phone-photos before exiting to the sidewalk, weaving
Between residents with loved pets and bags of supper food.

Perry Como

1.

I WASN'T THINKING OF PIERINO RONALD COMO from Pennsylvania with roots in Abruzzo or my Perry Como sweater, red with black-trimmed deep-V and three low buttons, which my mother bought for me when I was eight years old. I wasn't thinking about the TV singer or the sweater, but as Robert Frost writes, "way leads on to way," and Como leads on to Como, the vast lake north of Milan, our sight of the day to see. Midway on the route, the bus guide had us singing "That's Amore" and "Volare" from lyric sheets, Italian-American pop crossover hits from the late 1950s even if not Perry Como chart-toppers.

2.

AFTER HIKING THE STEEP SHOPPING STREETS of Bellagio in bloom, we motor-boated on Lake Como and passed George Clooney's villa. Word spread that he would be home if the shutters were open (they were) and his speed-boat tied at the landing (it was), just like the Queen's standard flying at Buckingham indicates she is in her castle suite. When all this transpired, it was as royal as a London palace, whether or not we saw him doing chores outside with his shirt off à la his pal Brad (which it wouldn't have been in the cool drizzle), and whether or not he sat with his wife, attorney Amal, on the lawn drinking a cup of Nespresso, which he pitches in Europe. That didn't keep the boat from tipping toward the shore as everyone leaned starboard to see, and our guide faked a call to his friend's cell.

Motor Ship Manifest

1.

"I WAS IN CHARGE OF CEMENT," Dale said when he got going at our table. From Nashville and before that Milwaukee, he's a retired military man and corporate manager. The cement work came in the army in Germany where he socialized with his counterpart officers whose fathers had fought for Hitler. Recovering from prostate surgery at seventy, Dale stays aboard with a suitcase full of disposable underwear. "I wasn't going to miss this trip. I'm a man who dreamed of sailing across the Atlantic solo."

2.

BART AND DOLLY FROM FLORIDA kept their house in Chicago when they sold his tool-and-dye company and left the Midwest. He retired at fifty-five and looks about twenty years past that, but Dolly is much younger than Bart's first wife, Lee-Ann, who died of congestive heart failure and a brain tumor sixteen years ago. A lifelong sailor, Bart had sailed on Lake Michigan and then captained a power-boat and a trawler out of Cocoa Beach. After he and Dolly married, they spent eleven months cruising the Grand Loop, the inland waterway route of eastern America, from Florida up the Atlantic coast to the Great Lakes and down to the mid-country rivers and back home through the South. Dolly navigated while he took the wheel and handled the lines.

3.

TWO FRENCH GUYS in their late fifties, one of them an eye doctor, the other an architect, on their honeymoon, both previously married—one with a son and two daughters. They come from the same New England town full of French Canadians, and their parents knew each other from the local golf club. They talked about a ninety-three-year-old woman friend, Helga, who had survived the World War Two fire-bombing of Dresden, Germany. They know her from their condo association in North Carolina where they vacation. A direct hit on her house killed twelve family members while she was two streets away looking for food. Helga fled Dresden at fifteen with a single potato in her pocket and in time found help at a U.S. Army camp where she was hired as a translator. There she met an American officer who fell in love with her. The man pursued the beautiful six-foot-two teenager, but she kept her distance, blaming his countrymen for destroying her family. Helga put the chocolates and oranges from the captain in a desk drawer. When she learned through German contacts that her father had been out when the bomb hit, she asked the American to find him. He did.

Pure Products

I have escaped from crazy America,
Sitting in a café near City Hall eating quiche
And drinking Swiss beer with Rosemary
On a Sunday morning in the August heat.
Green light-rail cars, washed for the new day,
Stop and go a few yards from our table.
The server, like others from Amsterdam
To Heidelberg, speaks English to us.

For William Carlos Williams, "The pure products
Of America go crazy." We're not the only ones.
It's often true, not always, but often enough
To slow us down when we cross the street
Or head for the next bend in the river.
I just want to sit for a while at a distance.

Wish You Were Here

Atlantic Corona

I only stared
       and did not
count the stars
       above our high
hill at five a.m.,
       air chilled and
the ground clear
       after straight rain
at year's end,
       but it's no
ending for the
       crown's spiky fit
here, eons from
       traveling light.

What's the Fog Like?

On the high hill in Amesbury, fog rises from lower woods
Like it's coming to get us with a light-gray net made of dew,
So fine that it floats, but that's not the exact word for it, so
Fine that it's another form of air, revealing the air otherwise
Invisible around and through us, the fog standing but not in
Fact standing, more like hovering and at the same time just
Inching up the former ski slope that will be discussed by a
Guest-speaker this week at the Italian eatery down the hill,
On the edge of the neatly preserved red-brick downtown,
The event hosted by the Bartlett Museum on Main Street,

Named for Josiah Bartlett, a doctor who was born here,
But is better known for being governor and chief justice in
New Hampshire after signing the Independence Declaration,
Which is why in his hometown there's a taller-than-life
Bronze statue whose butt-end faces one-way traffic due
To a revised road pattern that made a loop of the flow—
The fog like a lace shawl, a shroud, a weightless mist,
All the clichés in a million mediocre poems launched by fog
Banks, harbor fog, foggy bottoms, Foghat, and Sandburg,
The fog like losing my sight, losing the long view, an eye

Or two scaled over, straining to see past a milky filter,
The fog draining color from enduring pines and firs.
For ten dollars anyone can buy a ticket to the ski-hill talk

Coming up Sunday, by which time this morning's fog

Will have crept up and over our hill and been vaporized

By the guaranteed return of sun rays, if not today, then

For sure tomorrow, as April moves towards May and

Days of longer, stronger sunlight, the power that pulls

Buds out of winter sticks and green from the smashed

Bland grass on the favored powder-trail of past winters.

Other People's Postcards

Vic met me at the train. Having a swell time.
Seeing you people traveling the globe, I decided to try it!
If you don't write soon, I won't write anymore.
I'm at Salisbury Beach. Water is grand. You should be here.
The food really stinks in Berlin. Don't worry about me.
I'm having the trip of my life. Creation is full of wonders.
Well, some fun in the army. Will be a man when I get out.
We have one more day before going to Yugoslavia.
Montreal is nice, but I will be glad to be back home.
Every piece of ginger you sent was enjoyed.
Lorraine remarried 30 days ago, Junior living with me.
This trip is as close to paradise as I will ever get.
I'm fenced in with heat, rain, and Democrats in Providence.
This is the kid brother dropping a line to say I'm O.K.
Rio is huge, modern, and clean, and the beaches gorgeous.
Tell Dick we saw the Navy's Blue Angels stunt pilots.
Sent you a card to put in your scrapbook. I'm alive.
I just hate to go back to cold New England.
I was in Venice last year, too. Next stop is Trieste.
Arrived in Carolina Friday. Wish you were here.

Amtrak

The Hilltopper

The Southern Crescent

The Silver Meteor

The Cardinal

The Tidewater

The Niagara Rainbow

The Blue Water Limited

The Wolverine

The Palmetto

The North Star

The North Coast Hiawatha

The Lone Star

The San Francisco Zephyr

The Shawnee

The San Joaquin

The Mount Rainier

The Night Owl

The Bankers

The Adirondack

The Betsy Ross

The Minute Man

The Benjamin Franklin

Statue of Liberty Deli

Up in the tall green lady's crown,
I see Brooklyn and a ship in the Narrows,
And Manhattan, built puzzle with only inside pieces,
The story about millions of people hailing rides,
Heading for a million delis to order sandwiches,
Chopped liver on rye, with a pickle and Bubble-Up.

Dick Van Dyke

Past New Rochelle & the Pelhams, an Erector Set substation,
Knob-and-tube style with ceramic insulators on juice boxes,
The wound wires fenced with chain-link, a compact operation
Shipping a jillion volts to citizens who pay transmission fees,
Dozens of energizers along the railway in back of Eastman's
Corridor. Laura Petrie in capri pants needed a county lineman
And coal-fired amps to fill her shape in the face of cathode ray-
Bathed sectionals for two-point-five average kids. Mel Cooley's
After-image is tattooed inside our skulls. Web re-runs at 4 a.m.
Sourced Downtown per seat-back screen looping cooked data
Radiating from a tower, vectone inscribers pulsing. In skinny
Suit, soft hat worn in 1963, Oh, Rob, don't trip the circuit.

H for Huckleberry

"... instead of engineering for all America, he was the captain of a huckleberry party."
—Ralph Waldo Emerson on Henry David Thoreau

THE SAME WEEK that Rosemary and I visited Walden Pond for the water and sights, *The London Review of Books* marked Henry's two-hundredth birthday by looking at twenty new books about him and a national museum exhibition. Near the welcome center on state reservation land stands a replica of the writer's handmade cabin that he built in the woods. The original location calls the pilgrim from Concord or Tokyo who pauses and may toss a tribute stone on the pile. Under a hazy sky we placed canvas chairs on the narrow pebbly beach and set out towels and our books. Single swimmers made elegant lines in the middle of the pond.

Every few minutes another huckleberry-party captain led a small group of people up one of the trails into the surrounding tall pines and the oak trees whose helmeted acorns distribute themselves on hard-packed paths. Walkers see painted signs on stakes that add up to a kids' alphabet of things Thoreau, like "B" for the honey-makers that fill a niche in a system once overseen by the town's "self-appointed inspector of snowstorms." Lightning strikes and pickerel conventions were no doubt also among his supervisory tasks.

American Art

We were up to the Addison Gallery in Andover, Mass.,
Enjoying some famous Homer seascapes in the collection,
The black-and-yellow log cabin canvas by alum Frank Stella,
And a small Louise Nevelson with halved stair spindles,
As well as the model ships in the crypt, the lot of them
Like doll houses for men, precise and climate-controlled
In their jumbo cases, craftworks by retired captains,
The mother ships built in Boston or Newburyport,
Running the lanes from Liverpool to East America
Or down to Venezuela and back through the Antilles—
Before we stepped left into the library of blond wood
Whose walls held photo-documents of the nation's
Race war of the twentieth century, pictures by Gordon Parks,
James Karales, Ernest C. Withers, Stephen Shames: a young
John Lewis getting in the way just as he urges us to do;
Black men in suits with Allah placards; a pained Reverend King
Waiting to speak at the memorial for four girls murdered
At the bombed 16th Street Baptist Church in Birmingham;
One African American soldier headed to Vietnam;
And an image of a white woman in a dress outside a diner
Who is scolding a bunch of white men busy tormenting
Human rights defenders sitting in the street, a drama
Photographer Danny Lyon saw only once in those years,
According to *Memories of the Southern Civil Rights Movement*.
When the white men taunted: "Why don't you marry one?"
She sat down right there with the freedom fighters.

Boiled Potatoes

"Start the potatoes at five-thirty," my father would tell me
At ten past five when he left our house to drive downtown
To pick up Mum at the women's clothing store. Tonight,
I'm home with our dog while my wife is at Mass. General
Hospital seeing her mother's new knee. She took our boy
To Boston on his first train ride, telling me to start boiling
The potatoes at five-thirty because she would be back
At six with her dad and aunt for supper, which we eat together
On hospital days. There's thunder in the afternoon breeze.
Mum used to say, "When the leaves turn over, rain is due."

Nabs

Each time I open a package of the hazard-orange crackers,
I think first of my mother, Doris, who called them "Nabs,"
And then of myself as a college freshman between classes,
Feeding a vending machine. My wife says food that color
Must be toxic. Now, it's mother-in-law Mary with snacks
Fit for a brown bag, school lunch box, day camp pack:
My sorry choice, wrapped in cellophane weeks ago,
Loud like Longhorn Cheddar, glazed with peanut butter.
I chomp on what I shouldn't want, stubborn as my dad,
Who refused to see a dentist until he didn't need his teeth.

Memory Bank

I'M WAITING IN THE CAR for my wife to come out of the bank. For the next fifteen minutes, from every direction people crisscross the parking lot, waving at the white-haired cop who keeps traffic moving and cars from bumping one another. On the roof there's an electronic sign with the time and temperature alternating. If I didn't know this place is about money and saw the mix of women and men of different ages, as well as some kids, I might wonder what's happening. Nobody appears to take anything into the building; nobody looks as if he or she is carrying anything substantial out of the building. A few persons exit with paper in their hands, putting slips in their pockets. Several of them are eating pastry.

With my car window down, I hear what is being said in Greek, Khmer, Portuguese, French, and Spanish by people walking past me. I'm pretty sure they speak English, too. If I didn't know better, this could be a language school, citizenship office, or a ticket counter for ethnic events. Maybe these folks are trying to keep their native tongues, every Saturday going inside to say a few sentences to language teachers who reply, "Good work" or "Practice more."

It could be they are having their memories recorded or perhaps their dreams documented. Inside, they report what they recall about the old country and their journey to America. I might be all wrong. Maybe instead they describe a repeating nightmare, even reveal an explicit fantasy. A few of them show notebooks with scribbles kept on the bedside table. A clerk in the building catalogs the information and files it in a personal folder for future reference and later academic research.

It's some kind of local Cultural Depository here at the corner of Central and Middlesex streets. Inside, security cameras record them talking to the staff in low voices before helping themselves to jelly donuts and coffee.

New Boston Cemetery

Weathered squares of slate tilted in the ground—
Shoved by drifts, or maybe mourners hammered dirt
Until the stones budged. My crew and I visited
The settlers buried by war, birthdays, colonial flu.
They were away, at the end of a slim path
Ringed by a gray rock wall and bent iron fence.
The cemetery was a peripheral place,
Like the miracle shrine with its plaster saint
Filling a glass-covered case at my school.
Bus after bus of Catholics had come to pray.
The pastor hung cast-off crutches at a side altar.
By our first grade, the polio scare had faded,
But my classmates and I drank the oral vaccine.
One limping redheaded older pal ran over us
In games of tackle-no-equipment football
At a leftover farmer's field on Crosby Road,
And that visible evidence told much of
What we knew regarding pain and magic.

Common Ground

BLUEBERRY FIELDS TURN PALE RED, scarlet, crimson, rusty, the low-riding hills, low plants, scrubby Down East terrain rolling to the ocean, new-hayed fields, hay balers, tractors, roadside sign $20 per bushel of clams hosed clean for steaming—

Inlet sardine factory punched-out front splinters split beams broken teeth collapsed in back sagging roof gray rotten sills busted down and beside it a half-sunk old sardine boat white peeling hull gray boards decayed thru-out calm blue water in the cove—

Looking downhill the sun breaks into mirrors on the water blue pools blue ocean notched into this coastal section land slopes down to the sea a one-lane wooden bridge crosses low over shallow water orange maples by shiny red trees and golden-yellow leaves daub the partly green woods on all sides creamy tan grass in every field freshly cut acres sprout green whiskers Indian Summer—

Quart jars of maple syrup enormous pumpkins seaweed-infused bread whole-wheat bagels w/cream cheese mung bean salad country fiddlers Common Ground Fair Litchfield Maine south of Augusta goats w/ snipped ears giant draft horses pole-climbing horse-pulling solar collectors solar cells windmills wind-power fruit smoothies lemonade w/honey country women blue-denim & farm-dress women boots & braids women leancheeked tanned full-hipped clean-lined strong women shiny-haired women fiddlers and cooks and their men in dusty thirsty boots thick-haired pony-bound hat-topped with sunburnt arms reddened foreheads dirty bare feet pressed painter's white pants vest-wearing worn boots sheep-shearing book-selling alternative energy systems and structure designers all ages people one to one hundred at the fair carrots potatoes cukes zukes squash tomatoes all hung with blue prize ribbons families many young families w/babies in papoose pouches & carry-sacks & strollers or held by hand, led around the grounds past the animal auction nifty little goat kids small faces taller milk goats clean-washed goats some w/ears cut off beefalo beef cattle grass-fed cattle buffalo hybrids large brown cattle Shetland ponies long-maned crowds storytellers puppet shows weathermen a girl w/long skirt walking around on stilts like normal strolling—

Tents with exhibits books paintings pottery stained glass weaving macramé rugs etchings prints cane-work jewelry t-shirts literature & pamphlets natural food land reform childbirth info birth control info anti-nuke booth shelter institute insulation wood-splitting organic farming MOFGA Maine Organic Farmers & Growers Association organic seeds compost improvement beefalo semen rabbit cages pigeon cages sheep-shearing wool-carding wool-spinning thread-making yarn-spinning cloth-weaving spinners' circle spinning wheels pedal power ox teams sled rides human jukebox food stands hot dogs lamb-burgers tacos egg rolls o.j. vegetable Syrian bread sandwiches rice dish ice cream power tools farm machinery chainsaws lobster cart balloon man lost children announcements exhibition halls guest speakers Wendell Berry in the horse-pulling ring w/grandstand Helen & Scott Nearing yesterday talking about *Living the Good Life* Berry's *The Unsettling of America* the New Alchemists the American Friends Service Committee H.O.M.E. the Heifer Project Hunger International solar tents films slide-shows postcards wood stoves R-factor log-houses broad axe-hewn beams notched beams cordwood houses blacksmith Clivus Multrum ecological toilet hand-knit mittens w/red price tags shawls leather goods leather & lather show thermo-pane farmers police officers jammed parking lot people streaming in past a hairy guy asleep next to his dented guitar case with these words in red stick-on letters: HORN-SWOOP-ME-PONY-BUNGO-DOGSLED-ON-ICE

1977

Settlers

Turquoise sky the first day.
We broke ground with a rusty pick.
For a week, iridescent fish
Chased our flashlight sweeping the lake.
The next trip we dragged a pole up the road
To fly our flag.

We Looped a Winger

In the early morning movie dream
I was a Union officer traveling south on a train.
One car carried an unarmed work crew.
At a bridge we stopped to repair the track.
I noticed a sniper on the ridge—
Another man yelled, "Get the butterfly switch!"
I could see the switch but didn't know how it worked.

In another dream my father said to me,
"We looped a winger," describing how he and a friend
Drove all night from the Luray Caverns to Lowell,
Just before he and my mother married.

Kurosawa says, "All movies ask the same question:
Why can't people be happier together?"
A woman in the Sanctuary Movement swears,
"The Pope says we have a right to cross borders in search of life."

I used to worry about stepping on a nail.
How about a guy who won't tell you your coat's on fire?
I found a bottle of Moxie Nerve Food in the cellar of a mill.
Consider the bell as a public instrument
In the realms of work and grace and art.

Wool Grades: My Father's Notebook

—Marcel Marion, Stockton, California, 1967

Common Braid, 44's-40's

    ¼ Blood 56's

Mendocino

Black-Faced Lamb

    ³/₈ Baby

        Sacramento Line

Medium Burry

    Choice

        Humble County

Deadwool

    French

        Triple-A

Sonoma

    Fine Black

        Oregon

Tags, Cotts

        Super Choice

    Crutchings

Southern Wool

    ³/₈ Blood 58's

        Lamb's Wool

Fine Clothing

    Bux

Stuck with the Blanks

My brothers and I examined the small items our parents had saved. We had folded and packed Mum's clothes. The junk-drawer junk, linen, and bric-a-brac had been sorted. She had dealt with Dad's things eight years before. We were down to the fine grains. My father's war souvenirs were in the dresser: colorful campaign ribbons, Good Conduct Medal, dog tags that told us his blood type was "A." He'd kept a few issues of *Stars and Stripes*, the military newspaper, one with the headline: Hitler Dead.

She kept envelopes filled with holy pictures of saints. Mum was a "retreat lady" who believed what the Church taught and yet talked like the most practical Catholic you would meet. Dad had the crucifix he had worn at the junior seminary in northern New Hampshire, the same place he washed out of for reasons that remain mysterious to his sons.

In a 1930s notebook, he listed his reading, from Zane Grey westerns to the classics of French literature (in French). Not long after he died, I drove across country to California, a trip he had pictured taking. On the road he got as far west as northern Illinois on the highway when he and Mum visited number two son David and his wife, Dianne, and grandson Eric in the '70s. Going west, I stopped in Zanesville, Ohio, and thought of him reading those cowboy novels. There's a pencil portrait of

Dad in his twenties made by a travel companion. Later, a friend of mine said he resembled actor Ray Walston from *My Favorite Martian* on TV. In the 1940s, people said my parents looked like Vivien Leigh and Frank Sinatra.

We distributed Mum's jewelry to her daughters-in-law, sisters, relatives, and special friends except for a few pieces we could not let go. We found Mother's Day cards we had crayoned and decks of cards from a Lake Tahoe casino where she and Dad had vacationed. Her charm bracelet with a cable car marks the California years when Dad had been a sought-after tradesman working the wool co-ops in the Great Central Valley. In his diary from 1967, he writes over and over how much he misses his "Honey."

Richard said the personal effects seemed "thin," this collection of keepsakes. David surprised me, saying, keep what's left together, don't divide by three. Mum and Dad had clipped every news story about the three of us. They had been in the paper, too: one dark photo shows my father and co-workers taking a strike vote in the 1940s. He was a shop steward until the company broke the union by keeping the mill shut down. He rarely mentioned this. Another yellowed clipping reports that my family "chose Indian Head in the White Mountains and Hampton Beach in New Hampshire as their vacation spots."

What does it all come to? The German money and hammered gold earrings. The letter opener from Monticello. A golf tee and a store employee badge for "Doris." The blue diaper pin and Kennedy half-dollars. Ticket stubs from Fenway Park. The small bone-handled knife my soldier-father got in a trade for a can of peaches from a French farmer in 1945. Shoehorns and scissors. Eyeglasses, expired house keys, and matchbooks from fancy restaurants. The snapshots and birthday cards. The missing interview tapes and transcripts. We didn't write down the answers.

Twentynine Palms

This lady had a big loaf of
Banana bread in a plastic
Bag, which had to be in Twenty-
Nine Palms the next day; her
Son at a base there was leaving
For Japan. The postman said
Express Mail didn't go overnight
To Twentynine Palms, it wasn't
On the priority list, he couldn't
Promise. She asked about Special
Delivery. No good either. "Well,
Let's give it a try," she said.
"How much? Ten dollars, okay—
Don't crush it for Pete sakes."

Holy Ghost at Capo Beach

The padre in a black jersey and
Black pants rolled to his knees walks
Up the beach towards me, and a couple
He had embraced in the water stand,
Talking, in fog that could be souls.

Whale Grace

A jawbone frames the laboratory door.
Each winter, California grays plunge and run,
And laden watch-boats head out to spot a fluke,
A spray, any sign in the blue. This taking account,
This need to see, runs in us like the urge pushing
Giants south to calving lagoons. The totem
Is painted, carved, printed in the Orange County
Marine Institute, where bones of a whole
Creature float over murmuring aquariums,
The ribs arching even the town this festive week
While the big mammals, as they have for ages,
Slide by the chaparral bluffs from which men
Once scaled cowhides down to the beach for
Traders whose Boston ships worked this coast.

Water Man

He stops the Sparkletts truck near a palm tree
That looks like a pineapple and steps down—
His lemon-lime uniform glows, the tanned face
Whitens a smile, matching the look on the woman
In her yard, red shirt tucked into silver gym shorts.
She's been painting. The water man walks to the side
Of the truck and lifts out a large, clear plastic jug—
In one motion swings it onto his shoulder and turns.
The truck is filled with vessels, each with a sky-blue
Plastic seal. The back panel of the truck, all green and
Yellow fish scales, shimmers, shimmers, shimmers.

Salt Creek Beach, Monarch Bay

Surfers in black uniforms, nobody wears electric purple wetsuits,
specimens out of California central casting, lithe, beautiful,

sun-gold highlights in blond or blonde hair cut at a cool angle,
falling perfectly when soaked, guys and young women, a few boys

and some older men, one who looks like Tom Hanks in profile
carrying his board from the car lot across the street through the park,

its sloping lawn with basketball court, cement tables and benches,
built-in cookouts, lamp posts and dog-bag stations, no litter to speak of,

recycle-and-trash bins nearby, public access to the beach a holy right,
lots of runners in twos and ones along with pairs of walkers all ages,

the surfers do the surfer trot on the way to the water, a jaunty run,
not sprinting, hustling, small leaps in between, to the tide's edge wash

and then hopping three-four times, putting the board in and lying on top.
At noontime thirty surfers, most of them sitting on boards awaiting

THE wave of the next three minutes, there are always more, sun dialing higher,
and then, silently agreed-to, one of the surfers pops up, stands, grabs the top

of a bulging wave to skim it left or right depending on the break, squeezing
every gallon of foaming energy out of it, at times skipping off but more often

taken down in the collapse of the curl, a few with art-and-science skills
dance-step into a 360-shift and drain another ten feet of the ride, and then

it's back on the board, body surfing to the jumping-off point, all of this
by feel and look, no directional signs 200 feet from shore, a lot of waiting

as in making movies, patience, patience, patience, and then in a flash up
and sliding not walking on blue water, carving the run into the flow,

not much tube here but you can get more if you crouch and duck
under the natural break, the widening whitening liquifying arch.

The wave builds, fills to over-topping, spills at peak fullness and flips
itself forward curling into suds-wash like a billion champagne magnums

popping at once white and foamy, plenitude, the glassine plenitude
full to overfilled can't push itself forward another inch, runs out

its silver-blue string, the water translucent in the mounting roll,
light through wet bulge that smashes on itself in the slide

in the push from behind and gravity-pull to land to the edge of the water's
reach as far as it can extend this hour of this day, the tide clock run

by the moon's cosmic mechanism keeping time, keeping lunar time,
on the watch on the sea lane on the ocean drive, all these sets, wave sets,

sequencing in from what appears to be a mega wave machine on Catalina
Island that churns out hydraulic rolls like drill fabric sticking its long

and ever-longer tongue out of power looms in Lowell textile mills or red-hot
sheet-metal peeling off a roller in Pittsburgh or Tokyo steel mills, endlessly

rolling in, rather rippling in the long view, slightly heaving
in the medium-blue expanse, changing shape near the shore

where the tonnage runs out of room, sensing the finish line and
gathering up for the final push—why not make a splash?

At the wrap, light sees through, making a green glass
like empty Coke-bottles sheen for the finish, the lean-over forward

arching holding its form until the thing cannot contain the thing itself
and it comes apart comes ahead in a baritone bash, the crystal jade waterfall

falling over and sliding slapping itself in the face and bottom, up and down
its line the full length, now dissolving into airy agitated residue

in the shallows and running forward with its last gasp, turning
to stirred sea-soup soaking the beach until the scrap of its energy

plays out and reverses, and an opposite reaction draws the last of its
sauce back to the greater water where it mingles, gets consumed by

the oncoming rank—where does the end of the wave go?—just pushed
around in the last fifty yards all day?—the same final plunging water shoved

back-and-forth for the next hours until the whole business re-constitutes
at lesser tides, resupplying its aqua ranks for the next friendly coastal assault.

A pod of twenty surfers aligned on the tangerine-on-silver blue step-way from
horizon-slipping sun, sherbet-orange orb below mauve and rinsed gray layers

radiating from the sun north and south, the lines of pale raspberry and peach,
the sun taking itself out of the picture, the whole show a trick-to-eye with

Earth rolling ever so slowly out of line with the one true star of our lives,
all the sky-blue strips between apricot stripes turning deep watercolor azure,

the beach sand going blue, too, the wet patches of sand as sky-blue as high blue,
now gold burnishing yellow-gold washed-out layers under the plum shades,

violet shades, blended into horizontal mango smears, and the last blast
an electric-pink day-glo flamingo, a ten-percent slash between metal-flake

Pacific and the darker sky, the last surfers carrying boards up the beach,
a squeezed pink tube just where the sun was last seen as if the fire

extinguished its flame-pink, the end game of one more once, one more
planetary crank, the complete turning motion which is tough to get one's head

around, now pink-panties silk shrinking to a line, a magic bold felt-tipped
pen line that doesn't stay put but sharpens to a fine rule of peachy pink, soft,

a shadow of the red once there, striated, periwinkle crayon color, and brushed
wide strokes south-to-north, lighter toward Capistrano Beach and darker north

to Laguna, a relative sliver of rouged melon where the sun slipped into its slot
like a candy-wafer coin and not full round like the once-a-month orb overhead,

the moon this time rocking on its lovely curve, white nail-rind pinned up
on the unseen other seven-eighths so that the section illuminated gives no hint

of more to come, more at large, resting like a punched-out smile tilted goofily
to the right in a side-leaning head, a long white smile as if the lights are out

and you see the toothy grin—if you squint you can make out a smudge of
cloud around the lips as if there's a larger head or face obscured, a mask,

a face with a bag over, with a cut-out mouth lit from inside, but it's not Halloween,
a long way from jack-o-lanterns even though it's that attitude, that carved chuckle

under which crosses a helicopter, blinking red top and tail, on the way to Costa Mesa—
and for the surfers there has been no green flash to speak of or not speak of,

that secret private millisecond gem-green glint in the final fraction of sundown.

Lesser Antilles

Cool Blue

St. Lucia, St. Lulu, blue-green and green-blue—
There's an ooh in the blue air, in the o-round mouth
On the white deck of the cruise liner chasing a tank ship
Bound for the oil farm at Castries. Dark parts of the seascape
Like indigo ink slurred through turquoise fields in the bay.
Jet-lets of spume offshore: the dip boat, no banana boat,
Shipped out. Each villa boasts conch shells, T-Rex of seashells,
Grail we never find up north, bony case with smooth pink lining.
Each villa is a conch of white walls, terra cotta floors.
With its owner away, we snowbirds claim the showy chassis
For a few hot weeks. Julia, at the desk, says Nelson Mandela
Said if he had to choose a place to live outside of South Africa,
It would be St. Lucia, where he could sleep with doors open.
It's so calm, she says. Julia asks if my hometown is "cool,"
Calm, she says, not like busy New York City, where her sister lives.

Listening to George's "All Things Must Pass"

I'm on the Balcony notched into the rain-forest hill where the foil-blue sea seems to slide through railing posts, the steep angle tipping me toward the Caribbean, blue like the blue in my son's eyes that he got from grandfathers—the bay-caught blue smoothing west to the horizon, which is no end at all, just the curvy Earth meeting sky to join dark and light blue, a line that convinced early lookers of the far danger, the end beyond which the old maps warned "There be Monsters," for the edge appears to be there, even if always advancing, so the best sailor never falls off but will forever wrap navigational yarn around the blue-green ball, this sphere holding its own in bottom-free space, the forces and counter-forces swinging the unhinged globe around the hot-spot Sun in a delicate yet titanic dance among moons, broken asteroids, and fiery projectiles—the Sun the same and never the same, not stopped in time like my recollection of Sun Ray Bakery, whose short, fat, crusty loaves my mother bought each week and brought home in a white paper bag printed with the name of the shop around red sunburst logo, humble homage to our star, not so different from desert Sun worshippers, the Sun that does not rise or sink but flames in a self-published burn, flares leaping out of the atomic pot, crackling enough to scramble radio waves, Sun no more gold than the sky is blue.

St. Lucia Landing

All night the sea rolling its dough—
Near imperceptible thrust squeezing
A white curl from the end of its flat blue.
Moon's going to three-quarters, the stars sparse
As clouds push through the Lesser Antilles.
Fragment of one constellation—jagged line
Of light like decorated trees at Papa's Taverna.
The noontime sea will be such crystal aqua
All I'll be able to do is look, which is enough,
Not an easy thing, to just sit and look—
Even now I'm scribbling for you.
High on a volcano, cloud shadows shift.
Where the neck shot fury, smooth rock ages
On jungle trails west of Soufrière.

Cherry Tomatoes

Arthur's Cheese Tower

Behind the counter at the Paradise,
Arthur's peeling single slices
From a long block of American white,
Building a sticky tower, diamond-wise,
Which he places in the fridge.
It's local wisdom, a trade trick.
For the next grilled-cheese-with-tomato,
He'll life a slice, then another,
Picking each by an overhanging edge
To dress bread already griddling.

Lowell-to-English

The blue wash of cruisers signals some kind of injury.
Four postmodern kids, jazzed-up and famished,
Describe the crash as they walk in with us.

In the late-night lunch cart aglow in Formica and bright tile
Citizens dine on plastic trays.
We order fries and dogs with local dressing, the Works.

At the register, black moons the size of bagels.
There's a display of snapshots and news clips with quotes like:
If there's someone lying on the table,
Then someone's on the table."

We read the scene as we eat,
Conscious of the outside edge and our subtle intervention.
The more we talk, the more we change,
As slow as word-by-word translation.

What the River Brings

Among purple loosestrife
Spiking the river's stone grill,
Marie and I made out a figure,
Gray, face up. With chipped features
And blank base, the cast suggested
A park or church yard.
Exposed when the river retreated,
This weight must have come tumbling,
Immersed in the spring crest, muddy surge
Frightening all on the banks.
Days later, we returned, found nothing.
Flying saucers, hairy snowmen—
Bones that don't connect,
Dreams in a tense not invented.

Scouring Train

No adjective for the heat.
My olive-green t-shirt blackens
Before work starts on the scouring train
In the cellar of this mill.
I'm the keeper of the vats,
Three linked in a fifty-foot machine,
My train between two more.
A chute drops raw wool into harsh detergent soup,
Bubbling the shit out of it,
Then a big claw rakes acrid slop from vat one to the next
Until the whole mess hits the dryers.

Like an underground sentry,
I march up and down a yard-wide walk,
Using a hoe to unclog grates beneath each vat
Where steaming liquid strains into a wasteway.
There are regular red alerts.
When a section plugs, muck flows over,
And scalding soapy stew boils up,
I run down to scoop out crap.
The stink of cooked sheep dung, bleach, oil, and sweat
Makes me plan to burn my jeans at home.
With no fans, no relief,
And the sight of my twenty-year-man teacher,
I know there's no tomorrow.

Chinese Pie

Make sure your son knows about Chinese Pie, *Pâté Chinois*,
Baked by your *mémère* for her clan trooping home
To a winter kitchen warmed by supper and love.

She opened her window, while you, in your wife's land,
Surveyed the South China Sea, whose brilliance didn't speak
As fluently as your boyhood roads did at Christmastime.

Tell your son about the special dish, a kind of shepherd's pie
Layered with mashed potatoes, canned corn, and hamburg.
Who knows who named the concoction?

Scholars say Quebec settlers in China, Maine,
Copied a local baked dish and named it for the town.
It may mean something mixed up or maybe it's self-parody.

In 1881, a politician labeled the Massachusetts French,
"The Chinese of the Eastern states—
Industrial invaders, not a stream of stable settlers."

Attacked for loyalty to culture, the Canucks counterpunched,
And the next government report was kinder. You can order
Pâté Chinois in Montreal, one recipe the emigrants sent back.

A Hundred Nights of Winter

It's been so cold and bad
That it took until last week
To dismantle the public manger.
From my office window, through flurries,
I saw an orange dump truck pull away in traffic
With Joseph, Mary, shepherds, and angels
Standing crowded in the back like a bunch of refugees.
After a hundred nights of winter,
I'm ready to get out.

Nuts in the Mill

1.

DAVID WAS DOING some kind of Cajun two-step with white-haired Mary while carp jumped in the river below filthy windows. We ascended the east wall today, getting after the bricks with tools that clinked and conked. Sonia helped with her blues harp. Each brick is an orange and oxblood face under paint scales and soot, the lines, scars, and marks as true as any portrait. On the far bank, someone with binoculars could pick us out—dog-tired nuts dancing on the oily floor of a makeshift art school in the mill, potluck supper demolished, trash full of dead drinks.

2.

MY BROTHER RICHARD AND I worked side-by-side on the east wall this morning. He said it made him think of Uncle Bob and his brothers, who cleaned bricks for Blondie Patenaude at two cents each. There we were, fifty years later, across the river from our birth neighborhood, scraping bricks for the sake of art. Our uncles may have dreamt it, but would not have bet on it. Their sons and daughters, conceived under the river's influence, are scattered from Tokyo to the corner store, all of them sure they're past the need to salvage bricks for a few cents.

G-Room Energy

The upended

Brooms are

Cool torches

Burning with the

Fact of work.

Off-and-On Rain

The heat broke with a day of rain,
Off-and-on, like failing love,
The kind that skips logic from the humid start,
Having flared in a wink and carried on,
Burning a fuel stored in the body's softest parts.
Like a shower dousing zinnias and green tomatoes,
A break in human weather can rouse the sleepwalker.
Through screens comes the shushing of fat rain on leaves.
A little clearing, sunshine, then stillness and darkened sky,
A bass drum, and another round of rain—changing everything.

Odds

"If I make this light, she'll marry me."
Did I? I forget the results of my weird inventions
Put forth as divining rods.

Who isn't looking for an edge,
Hoping to get the jump on a disaster
Or trying to get that extra step to be ready
When a perfect chance drops in the lap?

Why don't our brains copy
Each precious instant of existence
(or maybe we don't know they do)?
If we could record each thrilling touch,
All the sights that make us talk,
That one mind-stretching sentence,
How would we act, wholly informed?

"But it ain't gonna happen," the wise guy says,
"Until we get to seventh heaven."
So, my best guess is that I made the bet two-out-of-three,
Speeding to the next intersection.

Design

Seeing the gray terrain,
I realized that landscape is only a start.

The forecast was fair,
So, I'd be drawing nails out of used lumber all day.

As usual, I'm the dreamer,
Waiting for sunset's amber slab.

I won't quibble over the price of twilight
Or wrestle with your generosity.

I'm nourished even as the hornets drill.
Let others worry.

Our seal must be significant.
Don't say there's no design.

Valentine

Red sweater
Slim frame
Warm breast
Open-hearted
Look of her
On the train
Opposite me
World passes
World happens
Looking into
Each other—
Her sweater
Her shiny hair
Bright heat of it
Soft wool of it
Put my face
Right there
Right now

Look at a Dry Leaf

A dry leaf is a physical map:
Riverbeds are sap routes forking off the prime vein.
While the underside is not printed,
The face is a bright terrain or scaly parchment
Resembling earth cracked by drought.
In one quadrant of this chart, locate red hills,
Check another for tracks of golden birch
Following tributaries south.
Like old maps, leaves curl and flake.
Oak is smooth brown leather.
Wine skin of a maple buckles.
A year-old leaf pressed flat makes a brittle dollar.
These small flags tell me: Autumn, North, Good.

North of Boston

Frost
Heaves

Travel Advisory

A big man on a big trip alone,
I yelled out the car window,
"I eat death for breakfast!"
And gunned the engine.

South Common Haiku

Train horn, no whistle,
Long into the cold and dark.
End and begin here.

The full empty pool.
Acres of after-effects
In the open field.

All kinds of plain threats
In and out of the shadows—
My spasmodic dog.

Over the low hill,
Whiff of Owl Diner bacon.
They serve oatmeal, too.

Creatures understand.
Left by the local falcon,
Rag of fur and bone.

Jungle-gym love perch
For a young couple at dusk
In their own middle.

Venerable tree,
Your shade has been long cast.
I have to go soon.

Who has not looked up
To see the white-thread jet trails
Which fade in seconds?

Holiday grieving.
Ancient popcorn carnivals
With plenty of salt.

In the early dark,
Memories of younger self
Waiting for a bus.

Martian Canals

Circumnavigation

Mile sticks add up on the highway.
Out here we whistle through the void,
Clocked and tracked by stations
That take us in their range and then
Give us over to the next link.
I'm over Micronesia—
It's like the archipelago of hope
Strung out from my gut through
Every hemisphere and time zone.
I want to taste you like the first time.
Last night, I dreamt I was in our kitchen,
Picturing myself at daybreak, bearded,
Legs cramped, eager for splashdown,
When my capsule, scorched from re-entry,
Would touch back in the rocking blue sea.

Field Experience

Years ago, when drifts were deeper and snakes bigger,
I wondered about the Earth's edge, the flat of the map,
And realized I was on the rim, the spot where a finger
Tapped the classroom globe. Outer space turned to sky,
Which became wind in the trees and then air in my lungs.
Fields were lookouts where once a UFO-watch broke up
When a white ship descended behind ten fleeing dreamers.
Corduroys whisking on busy legs, we'd sweep through hay
Toward frog-town in the swamp to peg rocks mindlessly.
Fields had snake-spit on saw-grass, the hum-buzz of bees
And milkweed pods, fish, we said, green bellies of feathers,
Oozing white juice when torn from their stalks.

We were roamers, unaware of the dust in our cells,
Gathering in fields for a better look at the constellations.

Camille Flammarion

B. Montigny-le-Roi, 2/26/1842

D. Juvisy-sur-Orge, 6/3/1925

Precocious, they called me, as if I were an early tulip,
When the doctor took my heavy book to scholars,
A work on the universe by the son of a Parisian farmer.
It's a long time since October ninth, 1847.
Doesn't every child remember a black sun?
I went for cloud formations at ten and volcano hearts later.
All the algebra got me into balloons, circus tents cut loose.
At my observatory in Juvisy, I obsessed over the red planet.
By then I was famous, my *Popular Astronomy* told people
What was out there. Go back to Mars, though—
The canals on the surface. Schiaparelli spotted them
Before hiding in Babylonian star-charts, before he went blind.
Those straight ditches aren't angel gutters. It's insane
To claim sole membership in a cosmos spiked with light.

Death Comes Home in the Morning

We got the word at work. Donna turned on the radio.
News came in the same tone as flashes from Dallas:
"President John F. Kennedy has been shot." We recalled
Twenty-three years ago, when we had one thing in mind.
While Ray and I ate lunch in the Dubliner, the TV was all talk,
No ads, and everyone looked up at the screen. It wasn't
The biggest loss in numbers, but it was a grisly end
And not supposed to happen. Our national machine broke.
Seven humans were gone in seconds, live death in the
Blue morning sky. And it wasn't supposed to happen,
Wasn't supposed to be that way for the believers who sing
"Sweet land of liberty" and tape a green dollar bill
To the wall in their first store, and wave each other on at a
Crossroads, the friendliest gesture between strangers on wheels.

Via Lactea

"We choose to go to the moon. We choose to go to the moon in this decade
and do the other things, not because they are easy, but because they are hard,
because that goal will serve to organize and measure the best of our energies
and skills, because that challenge is one that we are willing to accept, one we
are unwilling to postpone, and one which we intend to win."
—President John F. Kennedy, 1962, Rice University

WHEN I TURNED FIFTY YEARS OLD, I decided to try to keep up
with the Universe, that, and the world of high finance. It
was time to both take care of business and contemplate
the long view. What is "This" all about?

I bought a subscription to *Sky and Telescope* magazine,
which advertises "innovative astro-imaging gear for non-
gazillionaires," "sky sentinel cameras," "Nagler Zooms,"
"Dialectric Diagonals," "Truss-Tube Dobsonians," and
the "Celestron sky-scout personal planetarium," all
this on pages between articles about Dark Matter, solar
eclipses and lunar seas, meteor showers, the Sagittarius
star clouds, black-hole jets, cosmological enigmas, and
Mercury's orbit. One of my neighbors has a telescope on
a roof deck, but I didn't go down that shopping road. I
began reading more and watching "nature" programs on
television.

In my forties, I clipped news articles about space and
filed them in manila folders, which I marked with the

year, thinking they would be fodder for later writing. Who is the great poet of space? Who is the Walt Whitman of the Milky Way, the *Via Lactea* or road of milk as the Romans named it? In film, we have creative heroes of the Space Age like Stanley Kubrick, Tom Hanks, Carrie Fisher, Steven Spielberg, Sigourney Weaver, Ron Howard, and George Lucas. Tom Wolfe made *The Right Stuff* sail as nonfiction. Ray Bradbury, Arthur C. Clarke, Ursula K. Le Guin, Frank Herbert, Octavia Butler, and Isaac Asimov invented space worlds. Poet Tracy K. Smith, whose father worked on the Hubble Telescope, wrote *Life on Mars*.

In early 1997, the owner of a Lowell company specializing in polymer-coated textiles called me about a free-lance writing assignment. I wound up managing several days of media relations for the manufacturer of "the first man-made material to touch the surface of Mars," when the *Mars Pathfinder* bounced down on Ares Vallis of the Chryse Planitia region on July 4, 1997. NASA chose Bradford Industries, whose main business was coating car airbag fabric with silicone, to prepare material for a cluster of Vectran airbags to be deployed to soften the landing of the craft. They bounced fifteen times and didn't rip.

There was even a quirky tangent: nineteenth-century astronomer Percival Lowell of the "Lowell" Lowells in

Boston made news in his day when he claimed to have spotted canals on Mars. He posited that the linear surface features had been dug by Martian engineers. Later critics suggested that Lowell may have over-interpreted his observations of natural depressions in the soil because he was familiar with the extensive power-canal system in the textile-factory city named for one of his ancestors. *The Mars Pathfinder* held inside of it a robotic vehicle, a rover named *Sojourner* in honor of the well-traveled African American abolitionist and advocate for women's rights Sojourner Truth. The rover communicated with its designers on Earth until late September 1997.

On May 29, 1998, page one of the *New York Times* featured above-the-fold articles about Pakistan's underground nuclear tests, calling it the first "Islamic bomb," and a fuzzy digitized photo of radiating starlight above a small illuminated sphere described as "the first image of a planet outside our solar system." The location is the constellation Taurus, estimated to be 450 light-years from Earth. The Hubble Telescope made the picture of the planet, which could be twice the size of Jupiter, at the end of a 130-billion-mile path of starlight. The third story above the fold was a report about the federal Environmental Protection Agency announcing that automobile catalytic converters form nitrous oxide, which worsens global warming. Life is a chemistry set.

My son turned eight years old on February 9, 2003. When I was eight, Lt. Col. John H. Glenn, Jr., became the first American to orbit the Earth, and the Cuban Missile Crisis brought the United States and Soviet Union to the edge of a nuclear war. Government officials advised average families to build concrete fallout shelters in their basements to be prepared for a missile attack. The same year, Rachel Carson published *Silent Spring*, exposing the damage done to living things by the misuse of chemicals and probing the public conscience like a needle to the national brain.

Eight days before my son's eighth birthday, a NASA spacecraft disintegrated as it sped back to the Earth's surface. "The space shuttle *Columbia*, streaking across a bright blue Texas sky at about 3.5 miles a second, broke up as it re-entered the Earth's atmosphere," James Barron wrote in the *Times*. Everyone on board died: Navy Commander William C. McCool, the pilot; payload commander Lt. Col. Michael P. Anderson; Dr. Kalpana Chawla, an engineer; Navy doctors Capt. David M. Brown and Cmdr. Laurel Salton Clark; and the first astronaut from Israel, Col. Ilan Ramon.

Shift ahead: *Space News* in 2020 let us to know that the Laniakea galactic supercluster includes 100,000 galaxies. In that crowd is the Milky Way galaxy made of 200 to 400 billion stars of which the Earth's sun is one. There could be 200, could be 400, billion stars in our neighborhood. Billion.

Exeter Incident

"On February 29, 1860, Abraham Lincoln, having just given an electrifying anti-slavery speech at Cooper Union in New York City, arrived in Exeter, New Hampshire, to visit his son, Robert, a student at Phillips Exeter Academy."
—Exeter Historical Society

THIS ALL BEGINS with a 1965 report of a fast ship seen in Kensington, south of Exeter, a young guy and then a couple of cops claiming to have seen a flying "something" larger than the barn on the farm where swirling red lights came out of nowhere. We don't know how many people believed them. From this sighting emerged a yearly UFO Festival, a mash-up of local history, paranormal geekdom, and Chamber of Commerce good-fun circus with inflatable green spacemen, a saucer design contest for kids, and ultra-nerds speaking in the town hall where Lincoln spoke when his son Robert Todd studied at the town academy.

It's 2018, and examiner Bobby Terrio describes "Alien Encounters from New Tomorrowland," telling us that Walt Disney in the 1950s met U.S. Air Force brass to plan propaganda, a documentary movie meant to prepare Americans for the fact of galactic vehicles visiting Earth. Walt and his "imagineers" in Los Angeles had been promised exclusive use of secret government film footage of "real" flying saucers. The project got squashed—no explanation. Instead, Walt made a short film in the mid-'50s called *Man in Space* for his weekly TV show and later, maybe using UFO secrets he'd learned, built a robot president for the Illinois Pavilion at the 1964 World's Fair in New York, where crowds and I saw "Great Moments with Mister Lincoln," animatronic Abe on stage giving a short speech, timeless replica of the human in old Exeter, urging us to look for better angels in our future. Machine Lincoln lived down the fairway from *The Unisphere*, a giant steel Earth in mid-spin, illustrating how we balance on a ball and stand on the crust of one among countless launch pads in space, replete with unknowns.

The Local Void

[Imagine]

"You are looking at a region of mostly empty space 150-million light-years across called the Local Void. For perspective, the Milky Way galaxy is estimated to be 150,000 light-years across, making this void immense in its nothingness. Unlike a spiral or elliptical galaxy, the galaxy KK 246 looks like glitter spilled across a black velvet sheet. KK 246, also known as ESO 461-036, is a dwarf irregular galaxy residing within the Local Void, a vast region of empty space. This lonely galaxy is the only one known for certain to reside in this enormous volume, along with 15 others that have been tentatively identified. Although the picture appears to be full of galaxies, they are actually beyond this void, and instead form part of other galaxy groups or clusters. Cosmic voids, such as this one, are the spaces within the web-like structure of the universe wherein very few or no galaxies exist."

(NASA Goddard. Photo credit: *ESA/Hubble & NASA, E. Shaya, L. Rizzi, B. Tully, et al. May 24, 2020*)

Our Bodies

The atoms
In our bodies
Are old exploded stars,
A cosmic alchemy,
Still coming,
Whispering past
Shaggy galaxies,
Where tunnels of blue soup
Engulf crumbs of light.

A Dream of Perfect Games

The literature of sports dates from Homer and Ovid. Odysseus wrestled Ajax. Atalanta raced Hippomenes. The skater William Wordsworth "hissed along polished ice," and Marianne Moore said baseball is like writing: "You can never tell with either how it will go." John Updike's jump shooter has hands "like wild birds." Hundreds of years ago, in fields along the Merrimack River, Pawtucket and Wamesit peoples played games of speed and skill each spring when they gathered at the falls to fish.

—UMass Lowell Department of Athletics (1999)

Superman

Superman, Superman, fly right out!
Superman, Superman, fly right out!

And then one by one
Each drew a sneaker from the wheel of feet,

And when the last
Got stuck being IT,

The rest scrambled
To avoid the dreaded tag.

Such easy fun
As IT, laughing,

Wiped off the word,
Slapped it on another runner.

Releevo

AFTER SHORT-RECESS ON FIRST FRIDAYS, nuns pinned tissue hats on forgetful girls. From pews we praised God in song, reading from our missals, droning rosaries, professing our faith like small Apostles as the boys fingered marbles in their pockets, eager to play plunks or shoot for the bunny hole. We'd storm from the cafeteria to the dusty play yard under a sun glimmering like an altar paten.

We resumed our endless Releevo, a racing game in which we caught players and got caught, and in our fleet sneakers freed prisoners—Releevo! The trapped fled limbo, that in-between region, not heaven or hell, holding cell for imperfect souls waiting to be sprung. Quick kids tapped through the jail as fast as you'd flick a hand through fire, and everyone ran out toward more capture and salvation.

Canasta

You know what I mean.
You can't remember all of it.
Can't recall the details.
It was something you did way back.
Something you haven't done for ages.
You did it with people you liked.
And you could do it well.
Back then, you knew the rules by heart.
It wasn't a great big deal.
But it was something you did with others.
The memory is vaguely pleasant.
What are you doing now for later?

Minor League Poet

1.

Black-billed orange helmets on the dugout step.
The Stockton Ports dream of Orioles.
In choking heat, a farm team rides a bus
Down Highway 99 for a night game in Modesto.
Cool air blows around their heads.
One guy's eyes are playing tricks,
But he swears his slump is nothing.
The catcher wants back to Alaska.
Everyone else prays for a call from the O's,
A chance to quit the chalk-and-dirt routines
Of the Central California League.

2.

Dear Mary,
The balls are leaping off our bats.
Freddy is ripping it—a dozen homers this month.
Yesterday, we made the club's first triple play.
Jimmy grabbed a liner as he fell off the mound
And doubled up guys on second and first.
It's great to see us in first place in the paper.
I'm being platooned and can't get un-cranked,
But I did whack a double in Fresno.
Don't forget to write, if you have time.
Good to get mail. How's work?

Did you buy that car? Say "Hi" to your sister.
We'll be down your way next month,
So maybe you can make it to a game.
I'll have a day off, too. I miss you.
Don't forget to write.
Love ya, Tony

3.
Yeah, kids collected me.
I was number 328 in Topps' Series 5 in '66.
They took my picture while I posed at short,
Pretending to stab a grounder in the hole.
The card reads, "Bats right. Throws right."
That year I played 93 games for the Birds.
Year before I was up for two months.
Writers called me a utility man,
The spare at 2nd, 3rd, and short.
Had one homer, a high fly
That lipped over the Green Monster at Fenway.
Never was a pull hitter. Just yanked a hanger.
Next season I was sent back down,
Knocked around another while.
God, I'll never forget seeing that new baseball card.

4.

Hurry Harry, the hurler from Holyoke, Mass.,
Left mid-season to sell Bibles.
The skipper couldn't figure why he beat feet
After two good relief jobs in Greenville.
We said he got called up to The Show
To do some pitching in the Lord's League.

5.

Saw him at Triple Crown peak.
Carl Yastrzemski, Yaz, Yastro,
Potato farmer from New York.

The way he hitched
At his uniform
In the box,
And finally
Palmed the top
Of his helmet
As if giving
Concentration
One last twist,
Let us know
How serious.

6.

Slickery infield tarpaulin all puddled
After the blitz of exploding bolts.
Clubhouse bridge players hear:
"No game on account of rain."
Fans head for the exits.
Rain checks will sit in drawers
Until the Tigers return for a twi-nighter.

7.

Last Sunday in February.
Neighbors lean on sunny cars.
Snow pulls away from the grass.
At the corner variety store
Kids huddle out front,
Hustle off, scattering
Baseball card wrappers
Colorful as April tulips.

8.

Call the town meeting to order, Mr. Moderator.
Otis Ice Cream Palace vs. The Heron Chokers.
Lumpy field near Maggie's Camp—
Dead grass, cereal-box bases, junked car-hood backstop.

Regulars pull up on bikes, cycles,
In pickups and old vee-dubs.
Fifteen players, six gloves, and a dog-chewed catcher's mitt.
A couple-three cases of beer.

Total equal opportunity.
One pitcher wears combat boots. The bat's cracked & taped.
Talk about "Game of the Week"—
This is all beyond TV.

9.
I watch baseball in the lockdown
Cannot stomach political news
Tom Seaver and Lou Brock
Died a few days apart
The virus, dementia, cancer
This short season of Covid
Sucks pickled eggs in Boston
MLB Network fills my hours
Quick Pitch & Plays-of-the-Month
Brought to me by Gillette razors

Diamond Heroes & Villains

The following is an email message from October 2018 sent to my friend John Suiter in Chicago at 6:30 a.m., about three hours after the mythic contest between the Boston Red Sox and Los Angeles Dodgers ended with an 18th-inning victory in game three of the World Series. I quit watching TV after the top of the 15th inning when the Red Sox blew a good chance to break the 2-2 tie with at least one run. That was at 2:30 a.m. The game of over seven hours, longest in World Series history, began at 8:00 p.m. Eastern Time. I've loved baseball for sixty years, brought along by my father and brother David from the time I was four or five. For a time I dreamed of playing major-league ball, but I was not good enough to get beyond high-school baseball. I was the size of José Altuve and Dustin Pedroia minus the super-raw talent required for a short guy to succeed in the big leagues. I've followed the Red Sox all this time, watching them miss being champions until the now-legendary 2004 defeat of the dreaded New York Yankees and ensuing World Series win against the St. Louis Cardinals. The game last night and into this morning spurred me to tell John what I was feeling. He had sent me an email message from Chicago after waking up and seeing the game was still on. He wanted to know if I was up in New England and watching the action. Here's what I wrote to him—I added the title just now.

John,

IT WAS BASEBALL LIKE OPERA, like a Russian novel, baseball binge-watched in real time. I turned off the game after the top of the 15th when the main man Mookie (is he nicknamed for Mookie Wilson of the Mets or for Mookie in Spike Lee's movie?) took a whiff pitch with two outs and Jackie-Bradley-Junior on second. Backwards K. Our proven-MVP Mookie broke a record with 0-7 in a World Series game, matched by shortstop Xander B., 0-8. The top 3 slots for Red Sox were, like, 0-23. Terrible. But they had a chance to win.

I couldn't watch more. It was 2:30 a.m. The game did not end for another hour. I couldn't watch with all the horror movies of past Red Sox seasons in my head. Even with them up 2-0 in the World Series, I felt total dread. The sporting life is never safe for a Red Sox fan.

Nate Eovaldi. What a superman. He pitched a whole game, 97 pitches until he got stung by Max Muncy. Max. I think he was named after my recent story narrator, Max in Maine, in some crazy time-warp twist of birth in Texas or wherever Muncy is from. Maybe Trenton, N.J., where his mother slipped through a seam in a black hole and read my future short story on my website just before going to the hospital to give birth and name the baby Max. The new Kirk Gibson of LA-LA Land. 18th inning. Bottom. What more could Nathan do for us? Fly to Nathan's in New York and get that man a red-hot, a Coney Island, a foursome with onions, relish, and mustard as yellow as

Tweety Bird in the Sylvester cartoons.

Eduardo Núñez. A *Boston Globe* writer said he was in the wrong sport last night. The Bosox third baseman should have been in soccer shorts for all the tumbling, diving, and lurching he did from the 12th inning on. Is he dead yet? I was thinking after each of three falling-diving up-ends. A Facebook friend put up a clip from a Monty Python film with the knight missing two arms and a leg saying, I'm invincible.

The game was Boston's but for a skid in the near-outfield grass by 2b-man Ian Kinsler, who is what on the side? A bagpipes salesman? A kilt manufacturer? No, it turns out he's in business with rock star Jack White in Texas, making baseball bats called Warstic. But Kinsler, who got beat out for his college shortstop spot at Arizona State by Dustin "Pedey" Pedroia (who would go to the Sox), causing Ian to transfer to Missouri—Kinsler slips and makes a wild throw to first that never-before-playing-first-base Christian Vazquez (catcher) cannot haul in, not his fault—the throw goes wide to the photographers' corral. Run scores. Run scores. Tie game instead of a win for Boston. Nate must have died inside. Fellow pitcher Rick Porcello told the *Globe* he cried for Nate when it was over because Eovaldi left nothing on the field. An epic relief job. Magic Manager Alex Cora pushed him to the brink. 97 pitches. Leaving the scary Drew Pomeranz, lefty, sitting alone in the bullpen for what seemed like eternity, afraid to bring in Drew who could blow up in an L.A. Minute. It was Drew "Don't-Go-There" Pomeranz unless Nate had taken a line drive to the forehead. Even then maybe Cora would have made Brock Holt pitch. Brock-star has played everywhere else this year but catcher.

Oh, the pain. Insufferable *Globe* scribe Dan Shaughnessy with his insufferable tics (the Sons of Cora, like the Sons of Farrell and the Sons of every other Boston manager, plus his pop music name-drops) is already writing the obituary for the 2018 Sox. They were up 2 games, and now they are dog meat.

For 14 and ½ innings I watched one of the most magnetic baseball games I've seen on TV, even if only 4 runs scored at that point. They had me. The prospect of going up 3-0 vs. L.A. was not to be believed but suddenly possible before Mookie got whiffed and then the Sons of Dave Roberts hung in by fingernails until Max Muncy, let go by Oakland in 2017, blew a hole in the imaginary surreal HOOD dairy company blimp of Fenway Park fame floating beyond the outfield wall in Chavez Ravine, a stadium whose loaded origin can be learned in Ry Cooder's concept album of the same name that tells us about the working-class Mexican-American neighborhood that got bulldozed and wound up in hands of Brooklyn baseball money-men who brought their product to the west coast. But that's another story for another day.

Here, this morning, it's all hail Nate Eovaldi, the fallen almost-hero of the Carmine Hose who grew up in Alvin, Texas, also hometown of hardball god Nolan Ryan. Can you say "synchronicity?" Nate Eovaldi who came back from Tommy John surgery and pitched like Babe Ruth last night, the way the Babe in red socks pitched 14 innings in 1916 against the Brooklyn Robins in the borrowed Boston Braves field in Beantown. Nathan Eovaldi who performed under the Olympian gaze of Sandy Koufax sitting close to the field in a Dodger comp seat and looking like ten million bucks, a survivor of the Rat Pack-era who has kept his dignity and handsome looks. We remember Sandy Koufax. We will remember Nathan Eovaldi even though he got the "L" in game three of the World Series of 2018.

So, it's on to the field tonight after a seven-hour game. Ernie Banks used to say, "Let's play two," and they did last night even though unplanned.

Writing from the high hill in Amesbury, Mass., whose Main Street mural poet gave the name to Whittier, California, where the Quakers put down roots and up grew a toxic plant called *Richius Nixonium*, but that's another story. The Whittier Quakers of today were surely wearing Dodger-blue caps and rooting for Max Muncy at midnight. Root, root, root for the home team.

Au revoir, my dark hours correspondent.

Your fellow fanatic

The Fly

Fly leans back, his 650 Triumph growling up my driveway,
Flag gas tank and Captain America helmet from *Easy Rider*.
Each season he changed: on ice, the Golden Jet; Yaz, waving a bat;
Spinning to a hoop, Walt Frazier; and Tarkenton when launching
Autumn bombs to the local stand-ins for Homer Jones.

A red comb stayed hidden, a "foreign object" until he raked it
Across the skull of Big Time Wrestling lawn players,
Featuring Professor Tanaka, Bruno, and Chief Jay.

He tagged nicknames rapid-fire on a defenseless population.
Bill Buckley and Bee Gees mimic, he mastered the raspy mic
Of Boston Celtics' voice Johnny Most, who gargled gravel.
Fly won season's tickets one manic Boston Garden halftime
When he nearly blew a lung in a sound-alike duel, screaming,
"Havlicek stole the ball!" "Havlicek stole the ball!"

I met him in grade school, another short French Catholic.
One day on the bus he had clear plastic boxes sectioned-off
To hold turquoise rocks, pink quartz, mica, and pyrite,
The cream of his father's collection, for Show and Tell.

Catching Perfect Spirals

Trees change at night to yellow, orange, brown.
On warm afternoons my friends and I, boys and girls,
Raced downfield to catch every perfect spiral.
We tackled each other as if trying to hurt one another
When all we wanted was to be good at what we knew.
Red-gold leaves circled us. Our jeans got stained green.
We flung ourselves into the test, trying to prove our worth—
Each one measured against the other, but all stacked up
Against the worst the world could toss at us.
It's not enough to say it was a game in a farmer's field.
It was about order and chaos, playing by rules,
Teaming up to do a job, using strength and brains.
To call it joy makes it sound a little fancy,
But I still see shining faces and hear voices exploding
In the open air each time something went right.
We ran as if our lives depended on it, and who can say they haven't?
The moves I learned back then still drive me through the day.

Sweeney's Pond

Two SKATERS circled a large dark square swept clean of last night's dusting. I pulled my gear from the car trunk, slung skates over my shoulder, and stepped down the bank to the pond, the ice squawking to me. Snow ticked my face.

A father and son passed a puck, the boy maybe ten. I knew his dad, Ernie, as a kid when this place held marathon games. I joined them, shooting at a chicken-wire goal framed with 2x4's. A fourth player appeared and said he had lived nearby for twelve years.

He asked me, "Are you from California? I saw the plates on your Ford."

"No, I used to live down the street, just went away for a year."

We shed jackets and picked up the pace, snapping pucks at the goal. A jeep stopped, and another guy crossed the ice.

Ernie said, "You remember Mike from Raven Road?"

"Oh, yeah."

And Mike remembered me.

"I knew there'd be ice, but didn't think I'd see anyone I know," I said. "You guys still live here?"

"We'll be here for the rest of our lives," Ernie said.

"My brother and I shot a deer right back there, but we're losing the woods and fields to house builders. Good thing the area's a state bird sanctuary. Y'know Hudzik's farm? It's all houses from there to the New Hampshire line."

Then Mike said, "Time to get my own land. I've got money now. Had a bad accident at work. Lost an eye. See . . ."

He lifted sunglasses to show me the dead ball.

"Got a million bucks for it. Gonna buy land."

I asked about this and that person from years ago and where so-and-so had gone. In minutes, I'd tracked a dozen lives. A slapshot cracked my Sherwood stick. Snow let up. Sitting on lumpy swamp grass, I unlaced my skates.

"See you another time."

Skating

Pond ice, black as anthracite,
Inlaid with oxygen pearls,
The last words of fish
Before the cold snap.
Blue sun on my calligraphy.
Arcs and eights and yin-yang
Scratches on the glassy slate.
I'm lolling on freckled ice,
Orbiting hieroglyphs,
Marking fresh ice while school-kids dress.

Poetry Face-Off

In the spring of 2002 and again in 2004, my friend and poetry comrade François Pelletier of Montreal challenged me to a poetry competition tied to the results of the hockey playoffs between my Boston Bruins and his Canadiens. I joked that it was a poetry face-off. The one and only rule was that the loser of each game had to write a poem for the other guy in the winner's first language. That requirement broke down after a few attempts. Montreal won both series, so I wrote eight poems; François wrote five. Our friendly contest attracted the attention of the Canadian Broadcasting Company, which interviewed us live on radio twice during the 2004 series. In 2007, the poems were collected in a chapbook by Steak Haché, a literary magazine in Quebec, and ran through two printings. Four of my poems and two by François follow.

Silent Series

By François Pelletier

After four rolling-thunder games,
The one who appreciates most
The French silent broadcast,
"La Soirée du Hockey sans commentaires,"
José-the-Open-Door, says,
"Welcome to my net, dear Bruins' pucks."

Bergeron and Co. couldn't find words
To qualify his unwork.
All season, they yelled, "Theo is better
Than the Alexis Labranche of the goalies,"
Patrick Roy.

But playoffs are another season,
And we know WHO is
The Connie Smythe King.

Neighbors of the North

Before the referee dropped the first puck,
Bill Guerin's face appeared on the JumboTron
Asking Boston fans to respect the Canadian anthem
On this afternoon of all afternoons, when gloom
Fogged the Fleet Center after *L'Affaire Zednick*,
Source of hockey hot blood, bad blood, red blood.
The crowd did the only thing possible, considering
The Maple Leaf flag had recently draped
Steel caskets of four Canadian soldiers killed
Near Kabul by a "stupid" bomb from a U.S. jet.
Convinced that men on the ground were attacking him,
A pilot fired one of his "smart" weapons
With its billion-dollar guidance system.
He didn't know Canadians were training below,
Where North American friends, coalition partners,
Track Bin Laden among the ancient crags.
What does George W. Bush say to Jean Chrétien?
Guerin should not have had to request a courtesy
That should be a reflex, like Stanley Cup battlers
Lining up to exchange a good-will handshake.

François, Richard, & the Gang

Hockey will always be a game of speed not size.

José, can you see the Bruins' eyes tonight?

They will eat spoiled-pride sandwiches in the locker room.

They will replay mistakes this summer in the Laurentians.

They will curse bloody penalties taken in Montreal.

They will damn the linesman's late bad call on icing.

They will swear to bring earplugs next fall in Habsville.

They will not buy Canadian beer on the hottest day in July.

They will wonder if ZZZZednick's ghost put a spell on them.

They will suspect that Béliveau dropped a loaded puck.

They will remind fans that they finished first in the East.

They will try to forget that the playoffs matter more.

They will not wet their lips before kissing M. Stanley's cup.

Two Nothing to Four Over None

By François Pelletier

Théo the Falling Berlin Wall
Has learned another law of History:
There is no better winner
Against French Canadians than
Another Frogman.
Patrice Bergeron taught him
This lesson of North American Destiny.
Frog against Frog:
The coolest *batracien* wins.

"Watch out for Lapointe's bloody hits."

Foreign Canucks forget
The *fleur-de-lys* flag
When they see the net to fill
With their fluid shooting spirit.
Native-born mercenaries.

"Tu va-t'en souvenir de celle-là, Théo!
Et salut à tous les Bergerons."

Two nothing like two solitudes,
This could be a great tragical book:
The Rise and the Fall by Ourselves!
And we still wait for Kovalev's first goal,

But he is an empty-net scorer.

There will be no such occasion

With the Bruins during these playoffs.

The Fear of Waking History's Monster

There is no Boston loyalist born before 1960
Who does not respect the red-blue CH sweater,
The blue not the same shade of blue
That stuns Catholics in celestial Notre-Dame,
But rather a winter-scarf, cold Canada blue,
And the red like blood on snow, blood of a buck
Blasted by old Joseph Marion in a frozen field in La Tuque
In 1879, the year before he left for the red-brick mills,
Merrimack River Valley, New England, leaving for good.
He carried his past like a twelve-ton pack
Filled with every laugh, cry, and raw potato of confusion
He and his wife and their forebears had carried
Since the first of them made elegant line drawings
Of animals in caves in France before it was Gaul.
This history and modern stories of Serge Savard,
Jean B., Yvan Cournoyer, and J. C. Tremblay
Still haunt Boston hockey fans,
Especially French Canadian-Americans
Who loved the winning Bruins of long ago,
Even though they lacked familiar *Québec* names.
There were no families in my *Paroisse Ste. Thérèse*
Called Orr, Esposito, Hodge, McKenzie, Bucyk.
We feared men with names that resonated,
Rolled off our tongues like vocabulary words
In French class, names that matched lists

In the Sunday Mass bulletin, names we knew
To be the names from our northern tribe:
Cote's Market, Roy Fence, Lepine Realty, Gagnon Shoes.
But now the names in Montreal are beyond French—
Kovalev, Kovalev, the Russian, twice for two more goals.

Say It Ain't So, Sammy

We needed a bench full of Samsonovs
To battle the 20,000 zealots in *le Centre Bell.*
The only bear with a nose for the net,
Sir Sergei the Magician tried to stickhandle
His way to *la coupe Stanley* through a swarm
Of red-and-blue bees who must have had honey
On their blades last night, the way the puck stuck
And kept finding Canadian branches in Boston woods.
"Where have you gone Joe Thorntonaggio?"
Paul Simon could have sung in this series.
Théodore's quick glove and splits stopped
Most of the Boston bulls, *Olé, Olé.*
When Bégin smashed his face on the boards
And rushed back, sewn up behind Plexiglas,
To keep pounding Bruins in the corners,
We knew the *Québec* Crusade was true.
Boston could not rob the Hockey Treasury
Before the wide eyes of a screaming crowd
Standing on guard for M. Stanley.
Those crowd towels were not for crying
On the drive home to Rosemont and Longueuil,
No, the towels were for wiping spilled beer
From thousands of bars, dance floors, and dashboards
After the Mass ended and the faithful left in peace.
The struggle now returns to Boston,

Where the Gallery Gods and Beantown fanatics
Must channel the essence of Raymond Bourque
And "Exmozito," as *Pépère* Marion called Phil Espo.
Believers will scrape gold from the State House dome
To fortify the home uniforms of Bergie and crew.

Listening as a Sport

"We know it; we are time."

—Cavafy

On a day when Montreal ponds are giving up their ice,
The Air Canada jet banks low over the white stadium
Docked like a mythic ship on the old Olympics site.
The in-flight magazine touts the coming Athens games,
Contests that will enter the record in this jagged time.
In places like Lowell, pride will power interest. Greek
Or non-Greek, we'll be philHellenes 'til the flame recedes.
The most devoted fans will be the cultural regulars
Who fill city auditoriums, galleries, and school theaters.
They lean in to catch gestures and squeeze story-sponges
When they talk and teach. In a city of 100,000 souls,
Forty of the faithful take in a documentary about Sparta.
Eighty crowd a cooking lesson at a church festival.
Two busloads travel to New York to see Mycenaean art.
Hundreds praise a Greek-American piano prodigy.
They are the muscular memory workers—
As elite as Kenyan runners in every April's marathon.
Wave for these champions when the anthem resounds.

A Note on the Author

Paul Marion (b. 1954) is the author of *Union River: Poems and Sketches* (2017) and editor of Jack Kerouac's early writing, *Atop an Underwood* (1999). His book *Mill Power* (2014) documents the twentieth-century revival of the iconic factory city where he was born, Lowell, Massachusetts. With Tina Neylon and John Wooding, he edited *Atlantic Currents: Connecting Cork and Lowell* (2020), featuring writers from Ireland and America. His recent work has appeared in *So It Goes*, the journal of the Kurt Vonnegut Museum & Library in Indiana; *Café Review* in Portland, Maine; *PoetsReadingtheNews.org*, a national online publication; *SpoKe Seven*, a Boston-based poetry annual; *Résonance*, a Franco-American journal at UMaine Orono; and *Merrimack Valley Magazine*. With his wife, Rosemary Noon, he lives on a high hill in Amesbury, Mass., in sight of the seacoast and uplands of New Hampshire and Maine.